WEDDING
JEWELRY

WEDDING JEWELRY

30 *inspirational* *designs to make*

SIAN HAMILTON

First published 2017 by
Guild of Master Craftsman Publications Ltd
Castle Place, 166 High Street, Lewes,
East Sussex, BN7 1XU, UK

ISBN 978 1 78494 330 1

Publisher Jonathan Bailey
Production Manager Jim Bulley
Senior Project Editor Sara Harper
Editor Sarah Doughty
Managing Art Editor Gilda Pacitti
Designer Chloë Alexander
Photographer Laurel Guilfoyle (model shots);
all other photography by Sian Hamilton

Color origination by GMC Reprographics
Printed and bound in Malaysia

My thanks go to the GMC team who have been
(as always) a pleasure to work with on this book.
I would also like to say a huge thank you to my
biggest supporter – my husband Tony, for his
ongoing encouragement in all I do.

CONTENTS

INTRODUCTION

A wedding is the one time in a woman's life when she can wear a sparkly tiara or eye-catching headpiece and matching accessories with absolute confidence, knowing that she looks great. Wedding jewelry should effortlessly match a bride's own style, and what better way to ensure this than by making your own pieces?

Handcrafted jewelry adds a unique finishing touch that will help make your wedding day even more memorable without costing a fortune. The aim of this book is to show you a range of styles, from elegant and understated to dramatic, dainty, or bohemian. I want to inspire you to make imaginative, stylish pieces that will complement any bridal outfit. You do not need a lot of knowledge or skill to do this, just a bit of time and a lot of patience. Even if you don't see the exact style in this book that you are after, I hope that the special techniques and the clearly illustrated step-by-step projects will help you to turn your own ideas into fabulous wedding jewelry.

There is often a debate about sterling silver verses silver-plated metal for wedding jewelry. Tiaras and accessories for hair are often made with plated metals as they use a lot of wire, so can be very expensive if made in sterling silver. They also rarely come into contact with skin so there isn't the issue of skin reacting with the metals. Ultimately, the choice is yours. If making to sell, then you'll need to consider costs but if making for yourself, you might decide that sterling silver is worth the price.

Every bride should feel like a princess on her big day, and with the help of gorgeous wedding accessories she'll look like one too. I've always wanted to do a book dedicated to wedding jewelry and finally, here it is.

Sian Hamilton

THE BASICS

IN THIS SECTION YOU'LL FIND KEY INFORMATION ON THE tools, materials, and techniques required to make all the projects in this book. Always buy the best tools you can afford—the better the quality, the longer they will last. Familiarize yourself with any tools, supplies, or techniques you've not used before to gain the most professional-looking results.

TOOLS & EQUIPMENT

These following pages show the basic tools you will need to make the projects in this book. You may already have some of these at home, while others are readily available in hardware and craft stores.

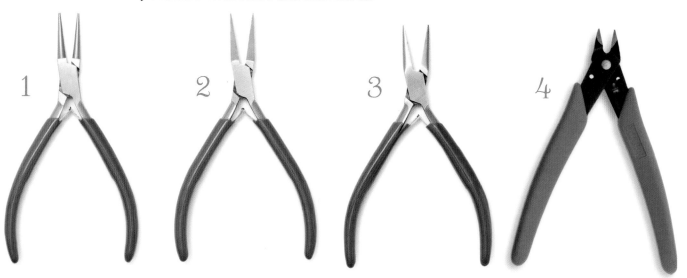

PLIERS AND CUTTERS

1 Round-nose pliers

These pliers have round jaws that taper at the end and are used for making jumprings, eyepins, loops, and spirals.

2 Flat-nose pliers

These have a wide jaw that is completely flat and tapers at the end. They are used for holding wire, closing ribbon crimps, and opening and closing jumprings.

3 Chain-nose pliers

Also called snipe-nose or half-round pliers, these are the most versatile type and are particularly good for holding small items such as neck ends.

4 Side cutters

These cutters have the cutting jaw on the side—they have a pointed nose and can cut flush to your piece. The point also allows the cutters to access smaller areas.

5 Scissors

These small, sharp, pointed scissors are used for trimming cords, ribbon, and thread, and for cutting shrink plastic.

6 Crimping pliers

These pliers are used with crimp beads. If you want to have a nice finish to your crimping then these pliers are a good investment.

Adhesive

When making jewelry, cyanoacrylate glues (known as superglues) are useful to help secure thread and wire on hairpins and tiaras—to stop hair catching when the items are worn. Silicone-based glue, such as E6000, is a thick industrial adhesive. This glue coats the wire, which stops sharp edges from scratching the skin, and is useful for sticking things to combs and metal findings. Always use adhesives in well-ventilated areas.

MISCELLANEOUS TOOLS

You may already have these at home as part of your jewelry kit or you can reuse household items.

7 Beading mats

These mats feel like velvet and have a texture that holds on to beads, stopping them from rolling around on the work surface.

8 Beading needles

Fine needles are available to use with beading thread. They come in several different sizes and are made to go through tiny seed beads with very small holes.

Measurements

While the conversions from metric to imperial are as accurate as possible, it is always best to stick to one system or the other throughout a project.

MATERIALS

The following pages will tell you all about the materials you need to complete the jewelry projects in this book.

EMBELLISHMENTS

You will need plenty of decorative materials for making jewelry for your wedding. Beads, crystals, and pearls should be extra sparkly and special for the big day.

1 Seed beads

There is a wide range of seed beads available in a rainbow of colors. These tiny beads are really useful in wedding jewelry to give a little bit of color or as spacers to separate other styles of bead. The most commonly used sizes are 1.8mm (size 11) and 2.5mm (size 8).

2 Crystals

Crystals are available as beads, pendants, buttons, flat-back stones, and montées (crystals in metal cups that can be sewn to fabric). They are beautiful and add sparkle to designs. Wedding jewelry often uses a lot of bicone-cut crystals, which have a faceted diamond or rondelle shape.

3 Pearls

Most of the pearls used in these projects are glass or acrylic as real pearls are very expensive. Glass and acrylic pearls have a pearl-colored coating and come in a range of colors and sizes. Acrylic pearls are lighter, so are good for pieces where you have a lot of pearls.

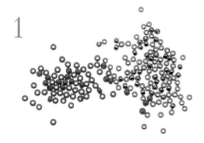

STRINGING MATERIALS, WIRE, AND CHAIN

There is plenty of choice of materials when it comes to stringing jewelry together. For wedding jewelry you will be using plenty of wire and chain, plus ribbon for decoration.

4 Nylon-coated wire

This wire is very good for stringing, as it has a better strength for heavy beads than ordinary threads. It also holds a nice shape on the neck. Nylon-coated wire is available in a range of brands.

5 Wire

Wire is essential when making tiaras because it's very versatile and comes in a variety of sizes. Wire is measured differently in the United Kingdom and the United States, usually being known as American Wire Gauge (AWG) in the United States, but normally referred to by its size in millimeters in the United Kingdom.

6 Beading thread

Used with beading needles for seed beading and beadweaving. The thicker threads can be used for bead stringing and secured with calotte ends.

7 Chain

There are many styles of chain and a variety of colors available. Fine chains have been used in some of the projects to make cluster jewelry.

8 Cup chain and connectors

This is a chain made up of small square cups with a rhinestone in each cup. It comes in a range of sizes and finishes. It works well for wedding pieces because it provides a high sparkle with little effort. Special connectors are available to allow the chain to be fixed to other items, such as jumprings.

9 Ribbon

There are many styles and sizes of ribbon available to use with jewelry-making. In this book, wide organza ribbon has been used for a wrap corsage-style bracelet.

10 Lace

There are many designs of beautiful lace available as ribbon or fabric. They work well as the base for wedding pieces, giving a nice vintage feel to the design.

11 Net

Net is used in combination with the lace to help strengthen the work and hold the beaded lace patterns in place.

FINDINGS

Findings are all the items you use to make jewelry that are not beads, pendants, or charms—all the essential bits used to hold your pieces together.

1 Jumprings

A jumpring is a single ring of wire that is used to join pieces together. Jumprings come in every size you can think of and many different colors.

2 Headpins and eyepins

These are pieces of wire with a flat or ball end (headpin) or a loop at the end (eyepin). Thread a bead on the wire and make a loop at the open end to secure the bead in place. Eyepins can be linked together to make a chain.

3 Earwires

Earwires come in various styles, from a simple "U" shape with a loop, to ones with a bead and coil finish. The loop is opened to take the earring piece.

HAIR ACCESSORIES

4 Hairpins

These are "U"-shaped pins that help hold styled-up hair in place. They vary in size and strength. When using them for wedding jewelry, look for the stronger ones.

5 Bobby pins

Bobby pins (called kirby grips in the United Kingdom) are a good alternative to hairpins if you need the hairgrip to hold the hair rather than just sit in the hair.

6 Tiara bands

These are silver or gold and come in a circle shape. They can be manipulated into a comfortable "U" shape to make them easier to wear.

7 Combs

Combs are available in metal or plastic and in a variety of sizes. They hold wedding jewelry pieces in place on the head and can be heavily decorated.

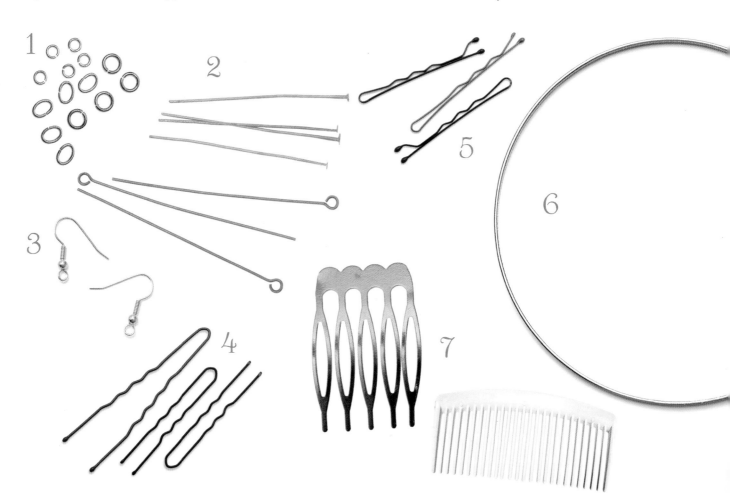

CLASPS

There are many different types of clasps. Choose one to match the style and design of the accessories you have chosen to make and wear.

1 Trigger

Also known as lobster or parrot clasp. These are the most widely used clasps on the market. Some come with a jumpring attached and they all vary in size and style.

2 Magnetic

These are great when making bracelets for yourself or for anyone who finds opening and closing clasps difficult. Keep in mind that magnets will attach to some base metals like plated chains.

3 Slide

This type of clasp has a barrel and loops on either side of the barrel. The barrel comes in two parts with one sliding into the other. Often the barrel has a magnet at the bottom to help it stay closed.

OTHER USEFUL ITEMS
4 Crimp beads and tubes

Crimps are used to hold your jewelry together. Crimp beads look like small metal beads with large holes. Crimp tubes are cylindrical. Use with crimping pliers to make a nice barrel crimp, or squash flat with flat-nose pliers.

5 Crimp covers

Used with crimp beads, these simply cover the crimp to make it look like a normal small bead. They come in a variety of metal color finishes.

6 Crimp ends

Crimp ends are another type of crimp used to hold your jewelry together and give it a professional finish. These are very easy to attach and hold securely.

7 Calottes

These are small-hinged cups with a loop on one cup, which can either be at the top opposite the hinge or on the side.

8 Sieves

These are shallow domes of metal with holes that you can attach decorations to. Sieves come as rings, brooches, or plain to attach to jumprings. They often come with a domed backing plate with small hinges to attach the sieve.

9 Brooch back/bar

This is a brooch pin on a bar that has holes to attach it to the piece being made as a brooch. It can be sewn on, attached with wire, or glued.

10 Shoeclips

Metal shoeclips are hinged in the middle. Half the clip goes inside the shoe and the other half is the backing for the decorated piece. They usually sit at the front of the shoe to add decoration to any plain court shoe.

TECHNIQUES

The following pages illustrate some of the basic techniques needed to make your own wedding jewelry and complete the projects in this book.

OPENING AND CLOSING A JUMPRING

To make sure that jumprings shut securely, it is important to know how to open and close them correctly. You will need two pairs of pliers with flat jaws—chain-nose or flat-nose pliers will work. If you find your pliers mark the jumprings, wrap a piece of masking tape around the ends.

1 Take a jumpring with the opening centered at the top and hold with two pairs of pliers. Holding the jumpring this way—with one pair of pliers across one side of the ring—helps to stabilize large rings.

2 You can also hold the pliers this way, with both pairs facing inward. Both ways are fine, and the way you need to attach the jumpring often dictates how you hold it.

3 Hold the jumpring on both sides and twist one hand toward you and the other hand away. This will keep the ring round in shape. Reverse the action to close the ring. Don't ever pull the ring apart as that will warp the shape. Use this technique to open loops on eyepins too.

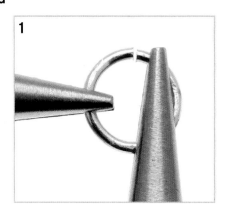

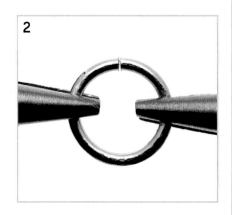

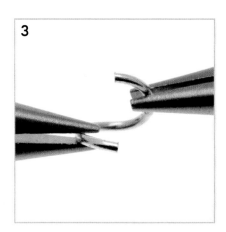

MAKING A WRAPPED LOOP

Loops have a multitude of functions in making jewelry, so making them properly is a skill worth mastering. This style of loop is the most secure. Once attached, it cannot be removed unless it is cut off.

1 Thread a bead onto a head or eyepin. Grip the wire with round-nose pliers next to the bead.

2 Bend the wire above the plier jaw to a right angle. You will need about ⅛in (2mm) of wire above the bead before the bend.

3 Move the plier jaws to sit at the top of the bend.

4 Use your thumb to push the wire back around the pliers, keeping it tight to the jaw.

5 Keep pushing the wire around the jaw until you meet the bead.

6 Move the pliers around the loop to hold it close to the open side and bend the wire around until it is facing out at a right angle. You should now have a complete loop.

1

2

3

4

5

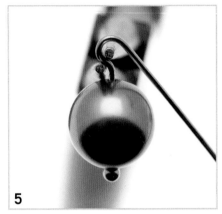

6

7 If adding the loop to chain or a jumpring, thread the loop onto the chain at this stage. Use a pair of chain-nose pliers to hold the loop firmly. Make sure any chain or ring is above the pliers.

8 Wrap the wire around the neck of the loop until it meets the bead.

7

8

9 Use side cutters to snip off any excess wire. Make sure the flat side of the cutter jaws is facing the coil.

10 Take the chain-nose pliers and push the cut end of the wire into the coil, so that it sits flush.

9

10

MAKING A SPIRAL

A spiral is a good alternative to a simple headpin to decorate pieces.

1 Take a length of wire. With round-nose pliers, bend the very tip around in a loop.

2 Place the loop flat in the jaws of chain-nose pliers and push the wire against the loop.

3 Work round in a circle, moving the loop in the chain-nose pliers. Allow the wire to coil around the outside of the loop to make your spiral.

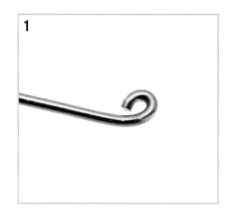

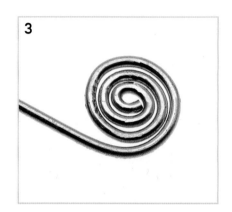

USING A CALOTTE

Calottes are used with beading cord to make a neat end for a necklace.

1 Make a large knot at the end of the beading cord. Thread the cord through the hole in the calotte until the knot is sitting inside the cup.

2 Cut off any excess cord above the knot and add a tiny drop of superglue, if desired. Using chain-nose pliers, press the calotte cup closed around the knot.

3 If the calotte has an open-style loop, then use round-nose pliers to gently form it into a closed loop.

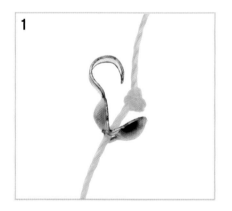

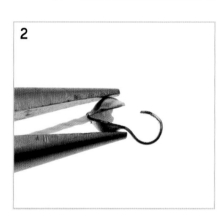

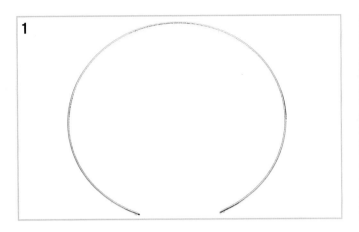

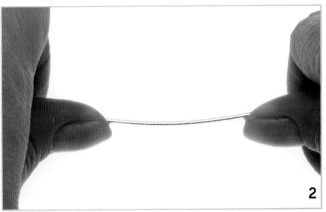

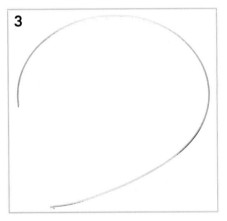

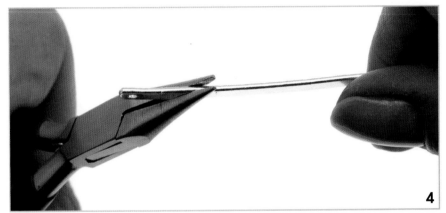

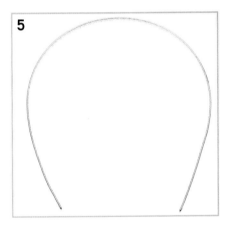

SHAPING A TIARA BAND

Most tiara bands come as a complete circle, so they need shaping to sit comfortably on the head.

1 This is how tiara bands normally start out; they have rounds ends and are about ¼in (5mm) wide.

2 Tiara bands are soft enough for you to bend with your hands. Hold the side of the band with your thumbs pressed against one side and your fingers on the other. Gently pull the band straight.

3 Work on one side first. Just straighten the side so it has a shape similar to a headband.

4 To straighten the ends you will need to use chain-nose pliers.

5 A good tiara shape will sit behind the ears or slightly back on the head and not move. It always makes sense to try the tiara band on before starting to work on the design. You need to feel it on your head, but it should not be so tight that it hurts. Be especially aware of the ends and make sure you cannot feel them pressing into your head behind your ears.

USING CRIMP BEADS

A crimp bead can be tube-shaped or spherical—they work the same way. If crimps are done correctly they will provide a strong hold for any type of stringing material.

1 Feed the crimp onto thread and create a loop by threading the strand back through the crimp bead. Hold the crimp bead in the pliers with the bead sat in the hole which has a round side opposite a "W" shape. The crimp bead should be level with the edge of the jaws of the pliers.

2 Before closing the pliers, make sure the bead is sat straight. If it's misaligned then the crimp will not close correctly. Press the pliers to squash the crimp closed.

3 Move the "U"-shaped crimp to the other hole in the pliers with two round sides. Turn the crimp bead so the "U" faces sideways to the plier jaws.

4 Press the pliers closed tightly. This will push the sides of the "U" shape together to make a tube shape again, with the thread trapped securely.

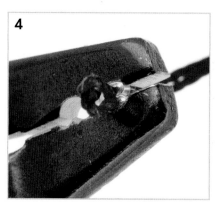

ADDING A CRIMP COVER

To give a professional-looking finish, it's a good idea to cover crimp beads with a crimp cover.

1 Take a crimp cover and place it over the crimped bead, making sure the bead is completely inside the cover. Take a pair of chain- or flat-nose pliers and grasp the cover either side of the opening.

2 Gently press the bead closed, making sure it closes completely with the sides together.

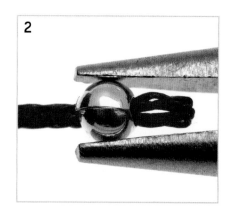

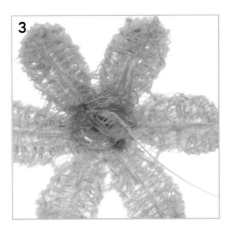

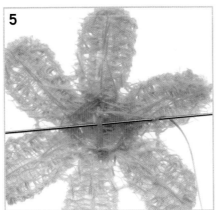

MAKING A SECURE KNOT

It's important to make sure you securely knot thread when you finish a design. You want to always finish on the back of the piece or in an area where the knots will not show. If working on something beaded then tuck the knots in between two beads.

1 With the thread exiting on the back of the piece, find a place where you can push the needle under a single or double thread that is already taut.

2 Take the thread and wrap it twice around the beading needle by the pointed end.

3 Holding the thread so it doesn't unwrap itself from the needle, pull the thread until the knot begins to close up.

4 Gently pull it as tight as possible.

5 Repeat to make a second knot. Doing a double knot will make sure it's completely secure.

6 Cut off the thread as close to the knot as possible.

Measurements

While the conversions from metric to imperial are as accurate as possible, it is always best to stick to one system or the other throughout a project.

CLASSIC
Collection

WHAT COULD BE MORE CLASSIC THAN WEDDING JEWELRY
made with pearls? The style is simply timeless and elegant.
Using both white and cream pearls gives a slight twist and the
variety of sizes adds volume. Real pearls can be very expensive,
so this collection uses imitation glass ones. If you want to splash
out, then look for genuine pearls—but do make sure that they
are real and not expensive fakes.

QUICK SIMPLE LOOPS

In this collection you will need plenty of beaded headpins with simple loops. These can be time-consuming to make, but this technique is a quick and easy way to produce them. The loops are not visible on the finished pieces, so they don't need to be perfect.

You will need

1in (25mm) silver-colored headpins
White and cream glass pearls
2.5mm (size 8) or 2.2mm (size 9) clear AB seed beads
Beading mat
Chain-nose pliers
Round-nose pliers
Side cutters

STEP 1

Place all the seed beads, pearls, and headpins that your project requires on a beading mat. Pick up a headpin and place a seed bead and then a pearl on the pin. Repeat to add one seed bead and one pearl to each headpin. Pick up one pin and hold it at the very end with round-nose pliers.

STEP 2

Roll the pin around the plier jaw until it hits the other jaw, then loosen your grip so you can rotate the pin and coil it some more.

STEP 3

Keep coiling the pin right up to the pearl. Now repeat Steps 1 to 3 for all the headpins on the beading mat.

STEP 4

Pick up the side cutters and a coiled beaded headpin. Place the cutters where the first coil on the pin crosses over with the piece coming out of the pearl. You need the flat side of the cutters facing the loop you are keeping so that you get the flattest possible cut on the end.

STEP 5

You should end up with a "P" shape. Repeat Step 4 for all the beaded headpins you need.

STEP 6

Using the chain-nose pliers, grasp the pin as close as possible to the end that's coming out of the pearl, and tweak the wire back so that the loop is sitting more centrally above the pearl. It doesn't need to be the exact center. Repeat this step on all the beaded headpins.

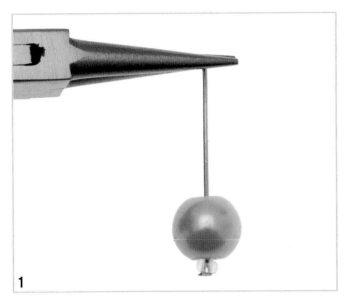

TIARA

Clustered pearls look great on a tiara and this is really easy to do. Mix up the sizes and colors of the pearls to add an extra dimension.

You will need

1 x roll of US 26-gauge (0.4mm) silver-colored wire
28 x 6mm white and cream glass pearls
25 x 8mm white and cream glass pearls
8 x 10mm white and cream glass pearls
5 x 12mm white and cream glass pearls
10g x 2.5mm (size 8) or 2.2mm (size 9) clear AB seed beads
1 x silver-colored tiara band
Beading mat
Superglue
Chain-nose pliers
Side cutters

STEP 1

Pick up the tiara band and shape it (see page 21) so that it is comfortable to wear. Cut a 40in (1m) piece of US 26-gauge wire (use shorter pieces if that is easier for you). Wrap the wire around the tiara band about 4in (100mm) up from one end.

STEP 2

Add an 8mm pearl and a seed bead to the wire then bring the wire around the outside of the seed bead and back through the pearl.

STEP 3

Hold the pearl close to the tiara band and pull the wire tight so that the seed bead draws up against the end of the pearl. Wrap this pearl in the center of the band. Wrap the wire around the band once to anchor the pearl.

STEP 4

Add another pearl to the band (you could use a 10mm one here) with a seed bead on the end. The process of adding pearls is the same for the whole design. Every pearl has a seed bead at the end and the wire always goes around the outside of the seed bead and back through the pearl. Wrap this pearl on the edge of the tiara band and wrap the wire around the band once to anchor the pearl.

STEP 5

Add more pearls using the same process as the last step. Mix up the sizes and colors (if using more than one color). Always wrap the wire around the band to anchor the last pearl added. Place the pearls on top of the band and on the edge.

STEP 6

The idea with this design is to not make it too neat and even, so let the pearls fall where they want. Don't worry too much if you have small gaps in the cluster, as those will be sorted out later.

STEP 7

Keep working around the band adding pearls until you have 4in (100mm) of band left. Wrap the wire around the band four times and cut off any excess wire. Press the wire end against the band with chain-nose pliers so it sits as flat as possible.

STEP 8

Cut short pieces of wire and attach to the band to fill in any gaps with extra pearls, where needed. When you have finished and are happy with the look, take the superglue and place a fine layer of glue on the back of the tiara band over all the wrapped wire. This helps keep it all in place and covers any sharp wire edges.

1

2

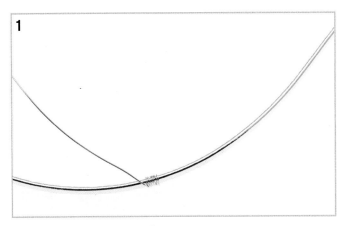

3

4

5

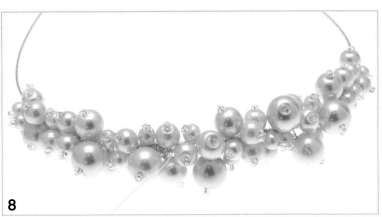

6

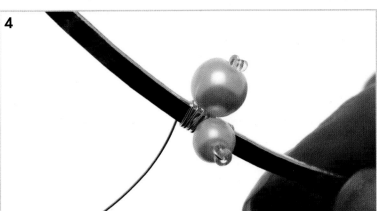

7

8

HAIRPINS

These easy-to-make hairpins look fabulous when the pearl pins are clustered in threes, but you can add more if you like.

You will need

- 1 x roll of US 26-gauge (0.4mm) silver-colored wire
- 24 x 6mm white and cream glass pearls (8 per pin)
- 9 x 8mm white and cream glass pearls (3 per pin)
- 6 x 10mm white and cream glass pearls (2 per pin)
- 10g x 2.5mm (size 8) or 2.2mm (size 9) clear AB seed beads
- 3 x hairpins
- Beading mat
- Superglue
- Chain-nose pliers
- Side cutters

STEP 1

Cut a 28in (700mm) length of wire and coil one end around the hairpin six times.

STEP 2

Add a pearl to the wire along with a seed bead, then bring the wire around the seed bead and back through the pearl.

STEP 3

Hold the pearl close to the hairpin and pull the wire until the seed bead sits tight up against the pearl. Wrap the wire end around the hairpin once and then around the base of the pearl.

STEP 4

Wrap the wire around the hairpin a few more times and add a bigger pearl and seed bead (pull the bead tight against the pearl). Place this pearl centrally on the top of the hairpin. Wrap the wire around the hairpin and the base of the pearl to secure it to the hairpin.

STEP 5

Add another pearl in the same way on the other side of the hairpin.

STEP 6

Add the next pearls in between the pearls already on the hairpin, filling in the gaps on the sides.

STEP 7

Keep going around the hairpin, adding more pearls to bulk up the shape. You should be able to push the pearls that you have already wired on a short distance because they won't be tight. Don't push them too far because the wire will snap.

STEP 8

When you are happy you have added enough pearls, wrap the wire around the pearls and in-between them to strengthen the piece.

STEP 9

Cut off any excess wire and tuck the end back in between the pearls to hide it. All these pearl hairpins will be a little different—don't get too stressed about them being perfectly matched as each one is unique. Repeat to make the other hairpins.

1

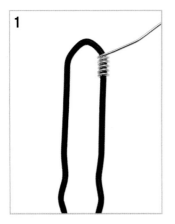

2

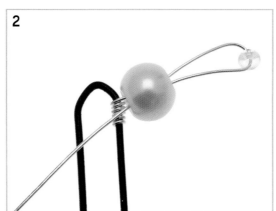

3

4

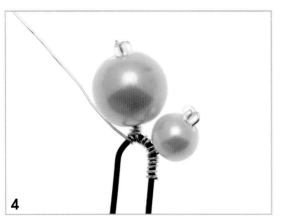

5

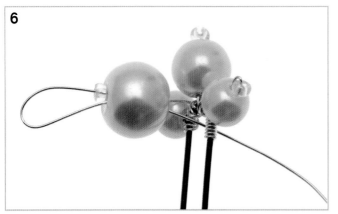

6

7

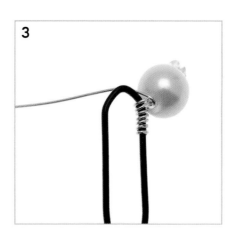

8

9

NECKLACE

This is a beautiful clustered pearl necklace made to sit high on the neck, by the collarbones. If you want to make it longer, add extra pearls to the chain and increase the length of beading wire you cut.

You will need

50 x 4mm white and cream glass pearls
31 x 6mm white and cream glass pearls
26 x 8mm white and cream glass pearls
2 x 10mm white and cream glass pearls
5 x 12mm white and cream glass pearls
10g x 2.5mm (size 8) or 2.2mm (size 9) clear AB seed beads
1 x roll of nylon-coated beading wire
66 x 1in (25mm) silver-colored headpins
2 x silver-colored crimp tubes
2 x silver-colored crimp covers
1 x silver-colored lobster clasp
1 x 4mm silver-colored jumpring
1 x 6mm silver-colored jumpring
Beading mat
Chain-nose pliers
Round-nose pliers
Side cutters
Tape measure

STEP 1

Cut a piece of beading wire about 16in (405mm) long. Thread on a crimp tube and bring the wire end back through the tube to make a loop. Pull the wire until the loop is large enough to take a jumpring. Close the crimp tube (see page 22).

STEP 2

Add a crimp cover (see page 22).

STEP 3

Thread pearls and seed beads alternately onto the beading wire. Start with a seed bead and then 7 x 4mm pearls, 5 x 6mm pearls, 3 x 8mm pearls and 1 x 10mm pearl, all with a seed bead in between.

STEP 4

Following the technique on pages 26–7, make up 66 beaded headpins using 20 x 4mm pearls, 21 x 6mm pearls, 20 x 8mm pearls and 5 x 12mm pearls. Thread all the beaded headpins onto the wire, mixing up the sizes and colors.

STEP 5

The pattern works best if you don't think about it too hard and let the sizes go on randomly—although you need to space out the 12mm pearls. When all the beaded headpins are added, the section should be about 3¼in (80mm) long.

STEP 6

Repeat Step 3 to complete the other side of the beaded chain.

STEP 7

Add a crimp tube to the beading wire and the 6mm jumpring. Bring the wire back through the crimp tube and pull until the loop is just a little bigger than the jumpring, so the jumpring is free to move. Close the crimp and add a crimp cover.

STEP 8

Finally, add the clasp to the other end using the 4mm jumpring (see page 18 for instructions on opening and closing a jumpring).

1

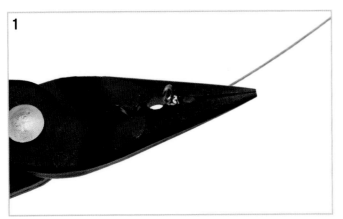

2

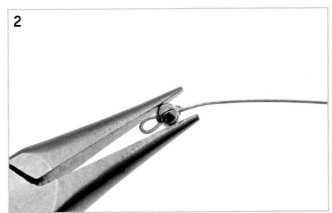

3

4

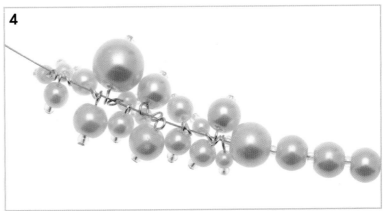

5

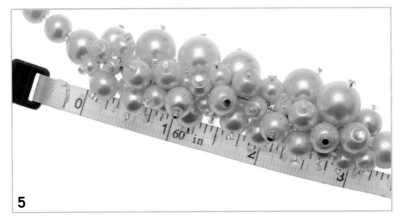

6

7

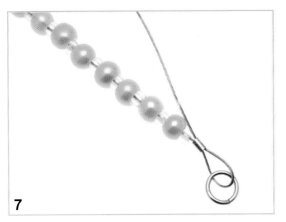

8

BRACELET

This lovely cluster bracelet is made up of different-sized pearls and seed beads attached to a fine chain. It is easy to make and looks very glamorous when worn.

You will need

- 10 x 4mm white and cream glass pearls
- 21 x 6mm white and cream glass pearls
- 16 x 8mm white and cream glass pearls
- 5 x 12mm white and cream glass pearls
- 10g x 2.5mm (size 8) or 2.2mm (size 9) clear AB seed beads
- 52 x 1in (25mm) silver-colored headpins
- 1 x 6½in (165mm) fine belcher chain
- 1 x silver-colored magnetic clasp
- 2 x 4mm silver-colored jumprings
- Beading mat
- Chain-nose pliers
- Round-nose pliers
- Side cutters

STEP 1

Using the glass pearls and seed beads, make up 52 beaded headpins following the technique on pages 26–7. Use one pearl and one seed bead per pin. You will have four different sizes of beaded headpins.

STEP 2

Add the magnetic clasp to the ends of the chain using the jumprings (see page 18 for instructions on opening and closing a jumpring).

STEP 3

Add a beaded headpin to the first link in the chain next to the magnetic clasp. Use the same technique to open the loops on the beaded headpins as you did to open the jumprings. Make sure each loop is properly closed before adding the next one. Add another beaded headpin to the next link. Then skip a link and add a beaded headpin to the next link along.

STEP 4

Keep going along the chain adding beaded headpins to links, missing out a link every few headpins. This will keep the beaded bracelet fluid and not too full. As you add the beaded headpins the bracelet reduces by about 1in (25mm) in size. The finished length of the bracelet is about 5½in (140mm), so the chain length should now fit properly around your wrist.

1

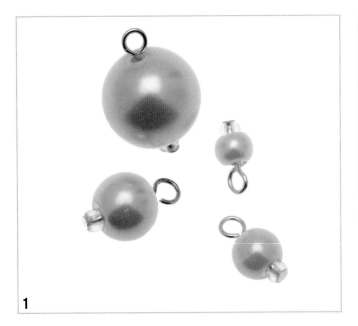

2

3

4

EARRINGS

These pearl earrings are at their most elegant when they are very long. If you prefer a shorter drop, they can be made to any length and still look stunning.

You will need

- 12 x 4mm white and cream glass pearls
- 12 x 6mm white and cream glass pearls
- 8 x 8mm white and cream glass pearls
- 2 x 10mm white and cream glass pearls
- 10g x 2.5mm (size 8) or 2.2mm (size 9) clear AB seed beads
- 34 x 1in (25mm) silver-colored headpins
- 2 x 2in (50mm) fine belcher chains
- 2 x silver-colored earwires
- Beading mat
- Chain-nose pliers
- Round-nose pliers
- Side cutters

STEP 1

Using the pearls and seed beads, make up 34 beaded headpins following the technique on pages 26–7. Use one pearl and one seed bead per pin. You will have four different sizes of beaded headpins.

STEP 2

Take the chain and add an earwire to one end. When opening a loop on the earwire or on the beaded headpins, grasp the loop by the open end and twist. Don't pull it outward as that will distort the shape. Twist it to open the loop and twist it back to close. Add a 4mm beaded headpin to the end link on the earring.

STEP 3

Add a 4mm beaded headpin to the next link in the chain. Skip a link and add another 4mm beaded headpin.

STEP 4

Skip a link and add a 6mm beaded pin to the next one. Then add a 4mm beaded headpin to the next link along. Skip a link and add another 6mm beaded headpin to the next one up. Miss a link and add another 6mm beaded headpin to the next one up.

STEP 5

Add a 4mm beaded headpin next then skip a link and add three more 6mm beaded headpins, each with one empty link between them. Add a 4mm beaded headpin, just above the last 6mm beaded headpin.

STEP 6

Above the last 4mm beaded headpin add the four 8mm headpins, spaced out with one link between each one. Finally, attach the 10mm beaded pin at the top by the earwire. Repeat all the steps to make a matching pair.

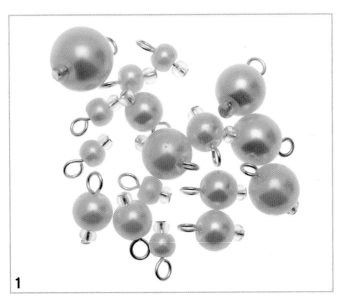

1

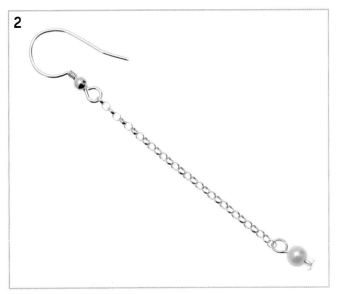

2

3

4

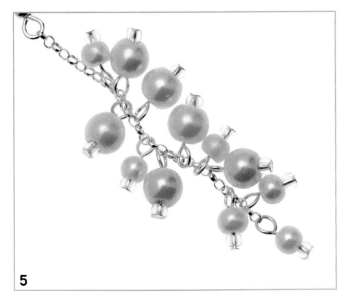

5

6

BROOCH

A clustered brooch makes a nice addition to a wedding outfit for a special guest and looks particularly good on a jacket. Have extra pearls available in case you need to fill in gaps.

You will need

10 x 4mm white and cream glass pearls
20 x 6mm white and cream glass pearls
10 x 8mm white and cream glass pearls
4 x 10mm white and cream glass pearls
10g x 2.5mm (size 8) or 2.2mm (size 9) clear AB seed beads
1 x 1½in (35mm) sieve brooch
Beading mat
Scissors
Beading thread
Beading needle
Chain-nose pliers

STEP 1

Thread up a beading needle with a manageable length of beading thread. Double the thread up and knot the end. Pick up the sieve part of the brooch and go through a center hole from the back to the front and through another hole to the back again. Pass the needle through the doubled thread and pull tight to secure the thread to the sieve.

STEP 2

Bring the needle through to the front of the sieve. Add a 10mm pearl and a seed bead to the thread, come around the outside of the seed bead and back through the pearl again. Take the needle through the sieve using one of the holes at the center. Pull it tight and bring the needle back through the sieve in a different hole.

STEP 3

Keep adding pearls with a seed bead, building around the sides of the first pearl added. Mix up the sizes.

STEP 4

Continue to add pearls until you have covered the sieve with some of the pearls around the edges.

STEP 5

Start to build up by adding pearls randomly on top of the first layer. Bring the needle up through the sieve anywhere there is a space.

STEP 6

The construction of this design is very fluid and can be as built up as you want.

STEP 7

When you are happy with how the brooch looks, bring the needle to the back and take the needle underneath the threads crisscrossing the threads already there. Knot the thread and cut off any excess.

STEP 8

To attach the back, line up the tabs on the pin section of the brooch with gaps in between the pearls.

STEP 9

Press the tabs down against the sieve using chain-nose pliers. Press each one until it is tight against the sieve.

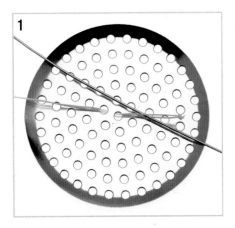

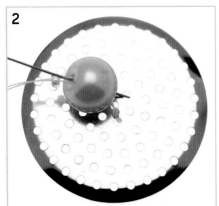

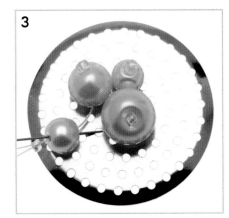

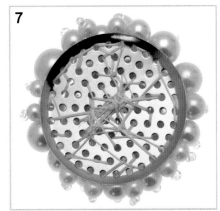

VINTAGE
Collection

THIS COLLECTION IS CENTRED AROUND EMBELLISHED antique-style brooches for a wonderfully vintage look. Your jewelry can be as ornate or a simple as you wish—just have fun trying out different combinations of crystals and pearls to go with the brooches you choose.

EMBELLISHING A BROOCH

This technique shows you how to add extra pearls to an imitation vintage brooch. These types of brooches are widely available and often come in multiple packs, so you can easily create a collection of pieces that match. Look for brooches that have lots of small holes in the designs to embellish to make the jewelry pieces unique. You may need to add more pearls if the brooch you are working on is bigger than 1¼in (30mm).

You will need

1 x antique-style brooch
6 x 4mm white glass pearls
6 x 6mm white glass pearls
Fine beading thread
Beading needle
Beading mat
Scissors
Side cutters

STEP 1

Remove the brooch pin, unless you are embellishing a piece that will be a brooch. If using a brooch of sentimental or financial value, leave the brooch pin in place and use removable findings so the piece can be easily returned to its original state. On imitation antique-style brooches the pins are often only held on with one soldered point, so it's fairly easy to pull the pin away from the brooch. Using chain-nose pliers, open the pin and roll the brooch pin base across the back of the brooch. This will break the solder join much more easily than trying to pull it straight off.

STEP 2

To add the pearls, thread up a beading needle with a doubled length of thread. Knot the end and cut the thread tail off as close to the knot as possible. Take a 6mm pearl and thread it on. Bring the needle through the doubled thread between the knot and the pearl.

STEP 3

Pull the thread tight and you should have the pearl attached to the thread. Move the knot so it's sitting centrally between the holes on the pearl. This is important so that the knot doesn't show on the finished embellished piece.

STEP 4

Pick up the brooch and decide where the pearl will sit. Take the needle through the brooch from the front and pull until the pearl is sitting up against the brooch. On this brooch there were small holes that worked perfectly to hold these pearls. Bring your needle through to the front of the brooch where the next pearl will sit. Hold the first pearl tight against the brooch by trapping the thread against the back of the brooch with your finger.

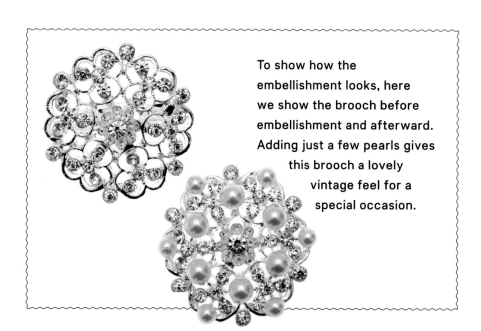

To show how the embellishment looks, here we show the brooch before embellishment and afterward. Adding just a few pearls gives this brooch a lovely vintage feel for a special occasion.

STEP 5

Add another 6mm pearl to the thread and bring the needle back through the brooch using the same hole that the thread is coming out of. These pearls are much bigger than the holes so they won't fall through. Repeat Steps 5 and 6 to add the other four 6mm pearls.

STEP 6

After you have added the last 6mm pearl, bring the needle through the brooch at the edge of the piece. Add a 4mm pearl to the thread and bring the needle down through a space next to the one the thread is exiting. To make this design balance, the 4mm pearls needed to sit in between two holes. Pull the pearl tight against the brooch and again hold it in place with your finger.

STEP 7

Add the other 4mm pearls in the same way. When you have added all the pearls, go around the brooch and through all the pearls one more time. This will help to keep the whole design tight and secure. Finish with the needle and thread on the back. Bring the needle under a thread (any one will do), make a secure knot (see page 23) twice and cut off any excess thread. If desired, add a tiny drop of superglue to the back of the pearls to keep them in place. This is not recommended for valuable antique pieces.

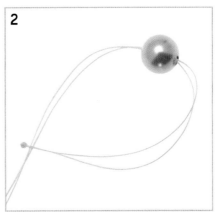

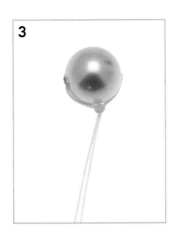

HEADPIECE

This classic bridal headpiece uses two matching brooches, but you could use one large brooch and one small one and place them asymmetrically on the head, if you prefer. If the brooches are already embellished, they can be used as they are. In this headpiece the brooch pins were left on the back so the jewelry could be dismantled and the brooches reused in the future.

You will need

2 x 1½–2in (40–50mm) antique-style brooches
2 x 1in (25mm) metal combs
40in (1m) x US 26-gauge (0.4mm) silver-colored wire
2 x 4mm silver-colored jumprings
2 x 6mm silver-colored jumprings
4 x 1mm by 2mm silver-colored crimp tubes
4 x 3mm silver-colored crimp covers
1 x roll of silver-colored nylon-coated beading wire
10in (260mm) x 3mm silver-colored crystal cup chain
2 x 3mm silver-colored crystal cup chain-end connectors
42 x 4mm white glass pearls
22 x 6mm white glass pearls
41 x 4mm bicone faceted crystal AB beads
7 x 8mm bicone faceted crystal AB beads
14 x 8mm rondelle faceted crystal AB beads
Beading mat
2 x chain-nose pliers
Crimping pliers
Side cutters

STEP 1

Pick up the length of cup chain and the cup chain end connectors. Place the end links in the end connectors and using chain-nose pliers push the two small tabs that are on either side of the connectors over the crystals. This holds them in place without the need for glue. Place to one side.

STEP 2

Make the pearl and crystal chains. Cut a 12in (300mm) and an 18in (450mm) length of nylon-coated beading wire. On both wires thread on a crimp tube. Feed the beading wire back through the crimp to make a small loop big enough for a jumpring to fit through. Close the crimp (see page 22). If there is an excess of wire beyond the crimp tube, cut it off with the side cutters.

STEP 3

For the shortest beaded chain, pick up the 12in (300mm) length of beading wire. Arrange 28 x 4mm glass pearls and 27 x 4mm bicone crystals on the beading mat. String them onto the wire alternately. You need to start with a pearl and this should mean you finish with a pearl.

STEP 4

To finish this chain, you need to add a crimp tube to the open end. This can be tricky when you have a chain full of beads, so to make it easier, thread on a crimp tube. Grasp the wire in chain-nose pliers and thread it back through the crimp tube. Push the wire through until it's gone past the end bead.

STEP 5

Move the chain-nose pliers and grab the wire sitting next to the end bead. Push the crimp tube as close to the end bead as possible.

STEP 6

Pull on the wire until the loop above the crimp is the same size as the one on the opposite end of the beaded chain. When you are happy with the size of the loop, close the crimp tube.

STEP 7

Add crimp covers (see page 22) over the crimp tubes on both ends of the chain.

STEP 8

Pick up the 18in (450mm) length of beading wire. For this chain you will need 22 x 6mm pearls, 14 x 4mm pearls, 14 x 4mm bicone crystals, 7 x 8mm bicone crystals, 14 x 8mm rondelle crystals. Arrange them all on your beading mat and follow this pattern. Start with a 6mm pearl, 8mm rondelle, 4mm pearl, 4mm bicone, 6mm pearl, 8mm bicone, 6mm pearl, 4mm bicone, 4mm pearl, 8mm rondelle. Repeat this sequence seven times. You should have one 6mm pearl left. Add this to the end and then follow Steps 4 to 7 to add the crimps and covers. Finally, add the 4mm jumprings (see page 18) to the end loops on this chain.

STEP 9

Pick up a brooch and open the pin. Take 12in (300mm) of US 26-gauge (0.4mm) wire and feed it through a hole on the brooch bar. Bring the end around to meet the wire and twist the ends together to secure the wire onto the bar. If your brooch doesn't have holes in the bar, then wrap the wire around the whole brooch bar.

STEP 10

Place the comb against the brooch bar and wrap the wire around both the comb and the bar to hold them together. Wrap a couple of times in between each tooth on the comb and move along to the next one. When you get to the end, cut off the excess wire and tuck the end around the back of the bar so it's out of the way.

STEP 11

Attach all the chains to the brooches. Take a 6mm jumpring and find a place on the right of one brooch at the side of the comb (at about 3 o'clock position) that the 6mm jumpring will fit through. Where this is will depend on the brooch. You may find you need a bigger jumpring if the brooch style is bulky. On the other brooch you need to fix a jumpring (at about 9 o'clock position) so it mirrors the other piece. Add the chains, using the shortest beaded chain first, then the cup chain and finally the long beaded chain, using the 4mm jumprings. Check the cup chain is facing the right way, then close the 6mm jumprings carefully so the ends are together to finish.

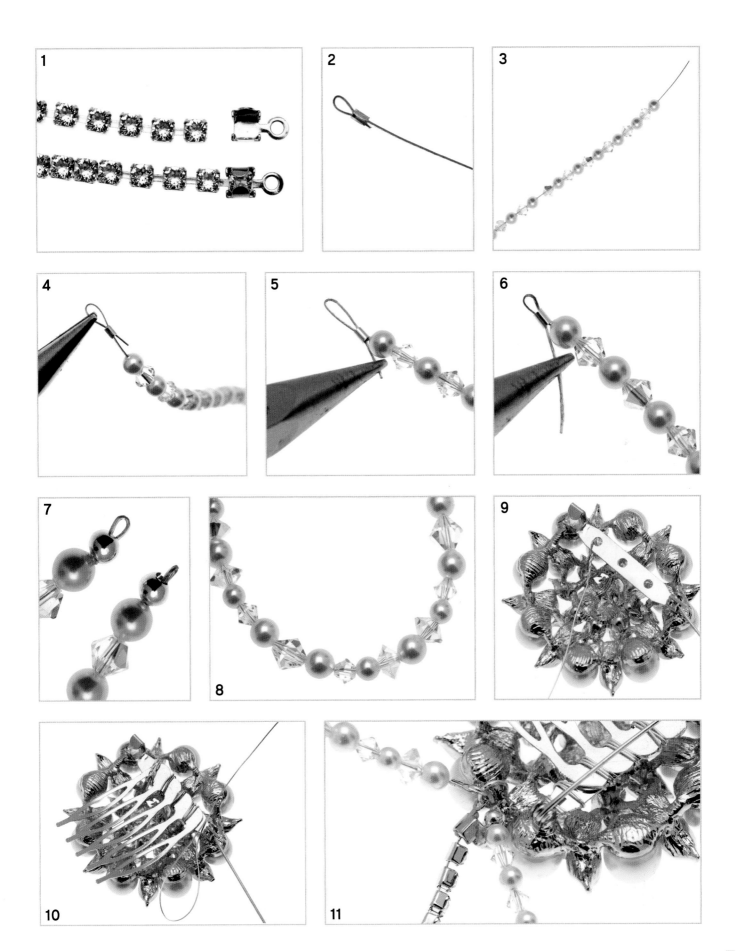

NECKLACE

This lovely necklace sits quite high on the chest. The shortest chain is about 16in (405mm) long, with the bottom of the focal pendant resting at about 17in (432mm). If you want a longer necklace, adjust to about 6 x 4mm beads per inch (25mm).

You will need

1 x 1¼in (30mm) antique-style brooch
1 x 3-loop magnetic clasp
12 x 1mm by 2mm silver-colored crimp tubes
12 x 3mm silver-colored crimp covers
1 x roll of silver-colored nylon-coated beading wire
114 x 4mm white glass pearls
48 x 6mm white glass pearls
126 x 4mm bicone faceted crystal AB beads
20 x 8mm bicone faceted crystal AB beads
Beading mat
Chain-nose pliers
Crimping pliers
Side cutters

STEP 1

Make up the pearl brooch focal piece by following the instructions on pages 46–7. Decide which way you want the brooch to sit; identify the top center. You need to think about where on the brooch you have places to feed wire through to attach the beaded chains. Cut six lengths of beading wire that are at least 12in (305mm) long. These will be longer than you need, but it's much easier to work with extra wire that you can cut off at the end. Take one piece and thread on a crimp tube, then thread it through the brooch. Bring the wire back through the crimp and pull until the crimp is sitting close to the brooch, but with enough room for the wire to move freely. Don't close the crimp at this point; just leave it open with the wire tail showing.

STEP 2

This first chain is the inside (shortest) one, so needs to be close to the center top of the brooch. A 4mm pearl marks the top center of the design. Remember that you need to mirror the beaded chains on either side, so make sure when you attach the first chain that there is a place to attach a chain to mirror it. Take 25 x 4mm pearls and 24 x 4mm crystal bicones and thread them onto the beading wire, alternately starting and finishing with a pearl.

STEP 3

When you have strung on all the beads, add a crimp tube and thread it through the end hole on one piece of the 3-loop clasp. Bring the wire back through the crimp and pull until the crimp is close to the loop but has room to move. Leave the crimp open.

STEP 4

Add two more pieces of beading wire to the brooch moving outward away from the center. Try to place these so that the three strands are as evenly placed as possible. Using Steps 2 to 4, add beads to the wires. On the middle chain you will need 21 x 6mm pearls, 11 x 4mm crystals, and 10 x 8mm crystals. Start with a 4mm crystal, then a 6mm pearl, 8mm crystal, 6mm pearl, 4mm crystal. Continue to alternate the 6mm pearls with 4mm and 8mm crystals and finish with a 6mm pearl. The outer chain is the same as the inside one; alternate 4mm pearls and crystals, using 29 pearls and 28 crystals.

STEP 5

When you have finished all three chains, close the crimp tubes (see page 22) and cut off any excess wire on both ends of the beaded chains.

STEP 6

Add crimp covers (see page 22) over all the tubes to give a neat finish.

STEP 7

Repeat all the steps to make the second set of chains for the other side of the necklace.

1

2

3

4

5

6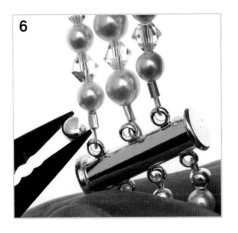

7

BRACELET

This bracelet with its attractive central brooch is about 7in (180mm) long. You want it to be snug but not tight, so that the focal brooch doesn't move around too much. For a longer bracelet, adjust the length to about six 4mm beads per inch (25mm).

You will need

- 1 x 1¼in (30mm) antique-style brooch
- 1 x four-loop magnetic slider clasp
- 16 x 1mm by 2mm silver-colored crimp tubes
- 16 x 3mm silver-colored crimp covers
- 1 x roll of silver-colored nylon-coated beading wire
- 42 x 4mm white glass pearls
- 26 x 6mm white glass pearls
- 32 x 4mm bicone faceted crystal AB beads
- 16 x 8mm bicone faceted crystal AB beads
- Beading mat
- Chain-nose pliers
- Crimping pliers
- Side cutters
- Tape measure

STEP 1

Make up the pearl brooch focal piece by following the instructions on pages 46–7. This bracelet uses a four-loop clasp, so you need to think about where on the brooch you have places to feed beading wire through to make the four beaded chains. The brooch will need to have space to attach wire on opposite sides of the brooch piece so it sits centrally with chains coming away from it on either side.

STEP 2

Cut eight lengths of beading wire at least 6in (150mm) long. These will be longer than you need but you can cut off excess at the end. You need to attach four pieces so that they sit nicely together and make the bracelet strap. Take one piece and thread on a crimp tube, then thread it through the brooch. Bring the wire back through the crimp and pull until the crimp is sitting close to the brooch but with enough room for the wire to move freely. Add three more pieces and make sure you are happy with the placement before closing the crimp tubes (see page 22). Cut off any excess wire as close to the crimp as you can.

STEP 3

As the finished length of this bracelet is 7in (180mm), each beaded chain is about 3in (75mm) from the clasp to the brooch. Start with one outside wire and thread on a 6mm pearl, 4mm crystal, 4mm pearl, 8mm crystal, 4mm pearl, 4mm crystal, 6mm pearl, 4mm crystal, 4mm pearl, 8mm crystal, 4mm pearl, 4mm crystal, and a final 6mm pearl. Add a crimp tube and attach to one end loop on the clasp. Leave the crimp open.

STEP 4

The next chain goes in this order: 4mm pearl, 4mm crystal, 6mm pearl, 4mm crystal, 4mm pearl, 8mm crystal, 4mm pearl, 8mm crystal, 4mm pearl, 4mm crystal, 6mm pearl, 4mm crystal, 4mm pearl. Finish with a crimp tube, leaving it open. Add the same beads to the next chain. For the final outside chain on this side of the bracelet, repeat Step 3.

STEP 5

On the other side of the brooch add the four strands of beading wire left over from Step 2. Repeat Steps 3 and 4 to add beads to all four wires and attach them to the other piece of the four-loop clasp. Leave the crimps attached to the clasp open.

STEP 6

Put the bracelet on and check that it fits nicely. It should be snug on the wrist, but not too tight.

1

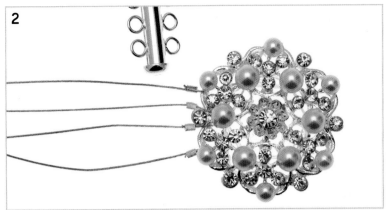

2

3

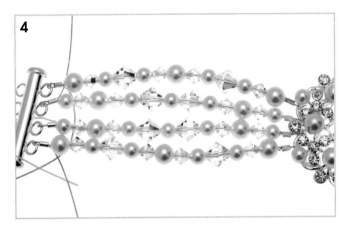

4

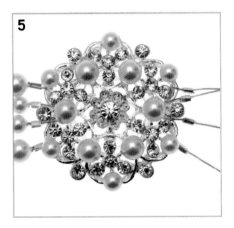

5

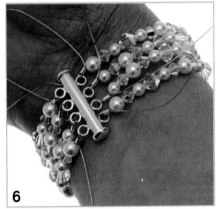

6

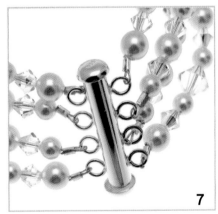

7

STEP 7

When you are happy with the fit, take the bracelet off and close all the crimp tubes. Cut off the excess wire.

STEP 8

Add crimp covers (see page 22) over all the tubes to give a neat finish.

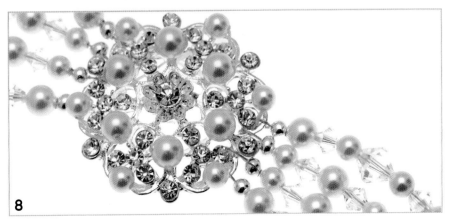

8

EARRINGS

Simple earrings with loops of pearls and crystals complement this collection perfectly. These can be hung from earwires or clip-on style earring findings that have a loop at the bottom. You will need to add two jumprings if you are using earwires that have a soldered closed loop.

You will need

- 2 x 1.5mm silver-colored necklace crimp ends
- 2 x silver-colored earwires
- 1 x roll of silver-colored nylon-coated beading wire
- 24 x 3mm white glass pearls
- 10 x 4mm white glass pearls
- 10 x 2mm bicone faceted crystal AB beads
- 12 x 4mm bicone faceted crystal AB beads
- White beading thread
- Beading needle
- Beading mat
- Chain-nose pliers
- Side cutters
- Scissors

STEP 1

Cut four pieces of beading wire about 4in (100mm) long. On two of the wires, thread on 6 x 3mm pearls and 5 x 2mm crystals. Start and finish with a pearl. On the other two wires thread on 6 x 4mm crystals and 5 x 4mm pearls. Start and finish with a crystal.

STEP 2

Take one of the wires with 3mm pearls and hold the ends together. Push the wires up through a necklace crimp end. Grab hold of the wires at the top (loop end) of the crimp end.

STEP 3

Take a wire with 4mm pearls and crystals and push both ends up through the crimp, so that this beaded loop sits below the smaller one. Wiggle them until they form a cross, so the smaller loop faces one way and the larger one is at a right angle.

STEP 4

When the loops are in the right place, use chain-nose pliers to press the crimp end closed. Press as hard as you can to make sure the crimp is closed tight. Repeat Steps 2 to 4 to make the second earring.

STEP 5

Gently give a tug on the beaded loops to make sure they are held in place. When you are happy they are secure, trim the wire ends off with side cutters. Cut one at a time, as you don't want to accidentally cut into the loop on the crimp end.

STEP 6

To cover the squashed bit of the crimp end (which can look a little untidy), create a ring of 3mm pearls. Thread up a beading needle with a length of beading thread; knot the end of the thread three times to make a big knot. Trim off the thread tail beyond the knot with scissors. On the earring piece, push the needle through the crimp end from the bottom and out of the side (by the side of the squashed section) and pull until the knot is hiding in between the beads at the base of the crimp end. Thread on 6 x 3mm pearls, push them up against the crimp and take the needle back through all of the beads again. Pull them as tight as you can.

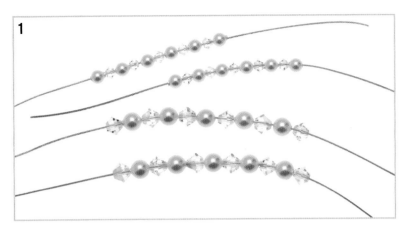

STEP 7

Underneath the six beads, wrap the thread around the crimp a couple of times to secure the bead ring to the crimp. Bring the needle through the thread and create a couple of secure knots (see page 23) to finish. Cut off any excess thread. Repeat Steps 5 to 7 to make the pearl ring on the second earring.

STEP 8

Finally, add earwires to both earrings. Take a pair of chain-nose pliers and open the loop on the end of the earwires by twisting it sideways. Thread on the loop at the top of the earrings and close the loop on the earwires by twisting it back in the opposite direction.

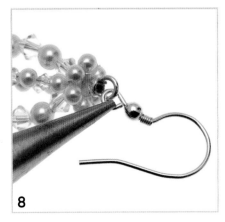

BROOCH

Brooches are a nice way to attach a buttonhole flower to a jacket collar or to add a little glamour to a simple wedding dress.

You will need

- 1 x 1¼in (30mm) antique-style brooch
- 12 x 1mm by 2mm silver-colored crimp tubes
- 12 x 3mm silver-colored crimp covers
- 1 x roll of silver-colored nylon-coated beading wire
- 4 x 2in (50mm) silver-colored headpins
- 4 x 6mm silver-colored jumprings
- 44 x 4mm white glass pearls
- 12 x 6mm white glass pearls
- 40 x 4mm bicone faceted crystal AB beads
- 2 x 8mm bicone faceted crystal AB beads
- Beading mat
- Chain-nose pliers
- Round-nose pliers
- Crimping pliers
- Side cutters

STEP 1

Make up the pearl brooch focal piece by following the instructions on pages 46–7, but leave the pin on the back. Cut an 8in (200mm) length of beading wire and thread on a crimp tube. Have the brooch facing you so that the pin is running horizontal and thread the wire through the brooch at the side, just above halfway. Thread the wire back through the crimp.

STEP 2

Push the crimp right up against the brooch, crimp it (see page 22) and cut off the excess beading wire.

STEP 3

Thread onto the wire, 3 x 4mm crystals and 2 x 4mm pearls. Start and finish with a crystal. Add a crimp tube then thread the wire through the brooch and back through the crimp. Check that the loop you've made sits right at the side of the brooch; if it doesn't, then pull the wire back out and try threading it through the brooch at a different spot.

STEP 4

When you are happy that it looks right, pull the wire so the crimp sits tightly against the side of the brooch. Crimp the tube and cut off any excess beading wire. Add crimp covers (see page 22) to both crimps.

STEP 5

Repeat Steps 1 to 4 to make two more loops of beads so they sit around the first one. The middle loop has five each of 4mm pearls and crystals. This one will start with a crystal and finish with a pearl. The outer loop has 8 x 4mm pearls and 7 x 4mm crystals. It starts and finishes with pearls.

STEP 6

Repeat all the previous steps to create the same set of loops on the opposite side of the brooch. Make sure they are balanced.

STEP 7

Make up four beaded headpins. Take a 2in (50mm) headpin and thread on: 4mm pearl, 4mm crystal, 6mm pearl, 8mm crystal, 6mm pearl, 4mm crystal, 4mm pearl. Make a wrapped loop (see pages 18–19) at the top of the pin. Make a second identical pin. For the shorter inside beaded headpins you need to thread on: 4mm crystal, 4mm pearl, 4mm crystal, 6mm pearl, 4mm crystal, 4mm pearl. Make two of the shorter ones. All the pins need to have wrapped loops at the top.

1

2

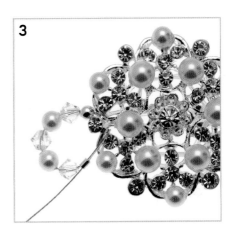

3

4

5

STEP 8

Attach all the headpins to the brooch
at the bottom, placing them so that
they hang straight and are even with
the longer ones on the outside. This
makes a shape that resembles a bow.
Use 6mm jumprings (see page 18)
to attach the pins; be careful when
closing the jumprings to make sure
they are closed tight with no gap.

6

7

8

COMB

This comb is made with wire to give stiffness to the bead arches so they stay in place. The comb and the brooch in this collection are interchangeable, so you can follow these steps to make a brooch pin instead of a comb. If you are making a brooch, don't remove the pin on the original vintage-style piece.

You will need

1 x 1¼in (30mm) antique-style brooch
1 x 1in (25mm) silver-colored metal comb
1 x roll of US 24-gauge (0.4mm) silver-colored wire
46 x 4mm white glass pearls
6 x 6mm white glass pearls
1 x 8mm white glass pearls
40 x 4mm bicone faceted crystal AB beads
Superglue
Beading mat
Chain-nose pliers
Side cutters

STEP 1

Cut a 12in (305mm) piece of wire and wrap it around the end of the comb, between the first and second teeth. Twist the wire ends together.

STEP 2

Fold the twisted wire end down the back of the comb and bring it through to the front between the same teeth again. Wrap the wire around once more so that it's completely secure. End with the wire facing up against the front of the comb.

STEP 3

Make up the pearl brooch focal piece by following the instructions on pages 46–7. Place the comb against the back of the piece. If using a genuine antique brooch, place the comb so it will sit comfortably by the side of the pin. Push the wire that is sitting at the top of the comb through to the front of the brooch and bring it back through so the wire comes in between two teeth. Wrap over the top of the comb and back through the same teeth.

STEP 4

Keep wrapping until the comb is secure. Be mindful of where the wire is sitting on the front of the brooch and try to keep it tidy, so it doesn't obscure the brooch design.

STEP 5

Finish wrapping when the comb feels secure and doesn't move. Cut off any excess wire and glue the wire end to the back of the comb. Try not to get any glue on the brooch!

STEP 6

To make the wire arch side sections cut a piece of wire about 4in (100mm) long and fold it in half. Press the fold closed with chain-nose pliers.

STEP 7

Add 2 x 4mm pearls and 3 x 4mm crystals onto the wire. Place them in the middle of the wire and bend it into an arch shape. You should have crystals at both ends.

STEP 8

Decide where on the side of the brooch the arch will sit and push the wire ends through from the front of the brooch to the back. Pull through until the beads are sitting up against the side of the brooch, then bend the wire ends to hold it in place.

STEP 9

Wrap the wire ends around the brooch once more and cut off any excess wire. Press the cut wire ends into the brooch with chain-nose pliers. Make another bigger arch using 8in (200mm) of wire with 7 x 4mm pearls and 6 x 4mm crystals; this time start and end with a pearl. Add this to the brooch in the same way so that it sits comfortably around the first smaller arch. Make two more identical arches following Steps 6–9 and add to the other side of the brooch piece.

STEP 10

Add two arches at the top of the brooch opposite the comb teeth using 8in (200mm) of wire for each one. The smaller arch has 6 x 4mm pearls and 5 x 4mm crystals; this one starts and ends with pearls. The larger arch has 7 x 4mm pearls and 8 x 4mm crystals; start and end with crystals.

STEP 11

Make one final arch for the top of the brooch, but this time don't attach it to the brooch. Use a 6in (150mm) length of wire and thread on 9 x 4mm pearls and 8 x 4mm crystals; start and finish with a pearl. Wrap the wire ends around the outer arches on the sides, between the first crystal and second pearl. Wrap twice and cut off excess wire. Repeat for the other end.

STEP 12

Add an 8mm pearl to the center of the arches at the top of the comb. Cut 4in (100mm) of wire and thread on the pearl. Move the pearl to the center of the wire and bend it at right angles on either side. Place the pearl where you want it to sit and, holding it in place with your thumb and finger, bring the wire ends through the brooch. Bend the wires up toward the pearl. Wrap one wire end around the brooch twice and cut off the excess.

STEP 13

Bring the other wire end through the pearl and wrap around the brooch. Cut off the excess and gently press the two wires coming out of the pearl together with chain-nose pliers.

1

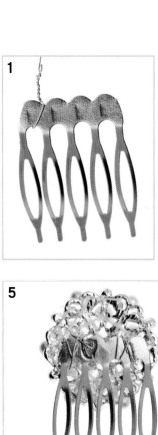

2

3

4

5

6

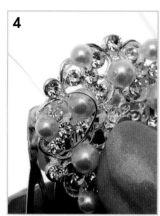

7

8

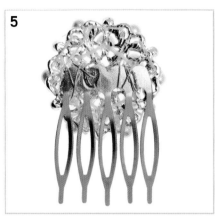

9

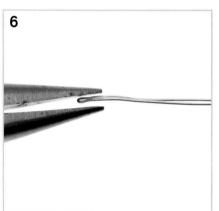

10

11

12

13

LACE
Collection

THIS EXQUISITE COLLECTION USES LACE FLOWERS AS THE base for delicate jewelry. The pattern of lace you buy will vary from the one shown here, but look for pieces to work on that are an enclosed shape—with an outside edge that you can cut up to. Attached to a piece of net fabric, the lace is sewn and embellished with pearls, beads, and montées. You can even make earrings using a tiny part of the lace design!

SEWING A LACE FLOWER

The lace you buy may be very different in style to the one shown in this collection. The technique for cutting out and sewing individual pieces of the lace pattern will still work whether your lace has a floral pattern or an alternative design.

You will need

Lace flower
Net fabric
12 x 3mm by 6mm white
   rice pearls (per flower)
17 x size 11 (1.8mm) silver
   seed beads (per flower)
1 x 8mm clear crystal faceted
   rondelle bead
Fine beading thread
Beading needle
Sewing pins
Beading mat
Scissors

STEP 1

This lace is a wide border style lace so has two rows of flowers in an open crochet style. Cut out a single flower with scissors (or whatever size piece the project steps say to cut out).

STEP 2

Cut a piece of net fabric twice the size of the lace flower, then double it over and pin the lace on top with enough pins to hold it firmly in place.

STEP 3

The edge is sewn with a stitch that goes over the side of the lace and through the net then back up through the lace. To start, cut a manageable length of beading thread, thread up the needle and make a knot at the end. Bring the needle through the lace from the back and pull to anchor the knot on the back of the design. Take the needle back through the net at the side of the lace.

STEP 4

Bring the needle back through to the front of the design a little way along the lace and pull tight. Continue in the same way all around the outside of the lace design so that the whole piece is sewn to the net.

STEP 5

When the lace is sewn on, you can take out the pins and then start to embellish with beads. If you have enough thread left, then bring it up at the base of one petal. Thread on a rice pearl and take the needle back through the center of the petal.

Lace flowers can be as heavily embellished as you like. If the wedding has a color theme, you can add matching seed beads to the flowers.

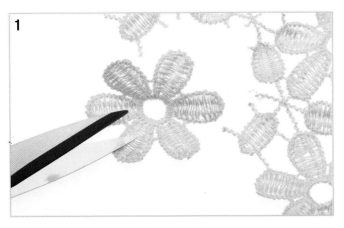

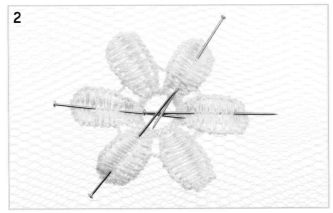

STEP 6

Bring the needle back through to the front at the end of the petal. Thread on another rice pearl and take the needle through the petal up against the first pearl added.

STEP 7

Bring the needle back through to the front at the base of the petal against the end of the first rice pearl. Then take the needle up through both pearls. Pull tight and take the needle through the lace at the end of the petal. Repeat this a couple of times to secure the beads firmly.

STEP 8

Repeat Steps 5 to 7 to sew pearls to all the petals. As your thread becomes too short to use, knot off the end and start with a new piece.

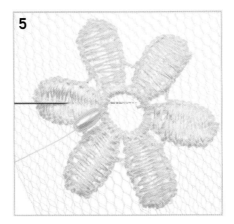

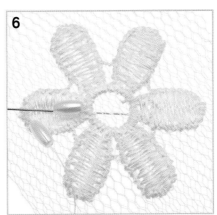

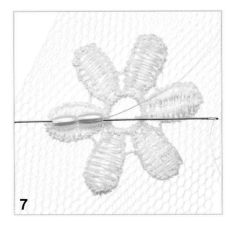

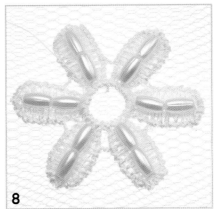

STEP 9

For the center seed bead ring, bring the beading needle through to the front of the lace at the base of a petal. Add a seed bead to the needle and bring the needle down through the lace the width of the bead away from where the thread exits the lace. Bring the needle back through the lace at the start of the bead and go through the bead for a second time; add another seed bead and again bring the needle through the lace the width of the bead away from the previous bead.

STEP 10

Bring the needle up to the start and go through both beads again.

STEP 11

Add another bead, go through the lace and bring the needle up in between the first and second beads. Go through beads two and three again. Each time you add a bead you bring the needle back up one bead back from where you are working. So each time you go through two beads, then add another one.

STEP 12

Keep going around in a circle adding one bead, then sewing through two beads until you reach the start.

STEP 13

Take the thread through all the beads again to make the circle firmer. The needle will go through about four beads at a time.

STEP 14

Bring the needle up through the center of the flower; here it's just net you are working with. Add the rondelle and the final seed bead to the thread. Go around the outside of the seed bead and back through the rondelle. Bring the needle back through the net at the center of the flower, but make sure you are not in the same place that the thread has exited. Pull tight so that the bead sits into the ring of seed beads.

STEP 15

Bring the needle up through the rondelle and seed bead again, then back around the seed bead and through the rondelle. Pull the thread tight.

STEP 16

If you are happy that the rondelle feels secure, then knot the thread off and cut off any excess.

STEP 17

Cut around the flower with scissors to cut off the excess net.

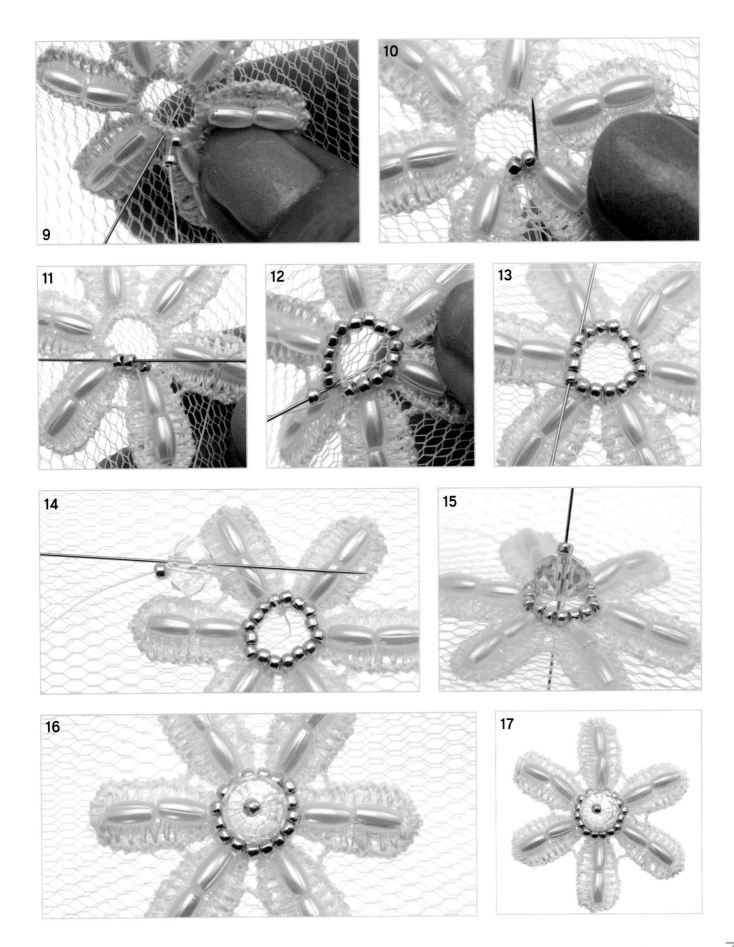

TIARA

This stunning design has a lace border with two rows of flowers in an open crochet-style design. If your chosen lace pattern is different, then use the steps to help you embellish your lace and attach it to a tiara band.

You will need

3¼in x 7in (80mm x 180mm) minimum piece of lace
Net fabric twice the size of the lace
72 x 3mm by 6mm white rice pearls
5 x 10mm by 4mm white rice pearls
10g x size 11 (1.8mm) silver seed beads
4 x 8mm clear crystal faceted rondelle beads
2 x 8mm white round glass pearls
2 x 4mm crystal montées
Silver-colored tiara band
Fine beading thread
Beading needle
Sewing pins
Beading mat
Scissors

STEP 1

Cut out and sew around the flower shape following Steps 1 to 4 of the technique on pages 68–71. Bring the needle up through the lace on the center oval. Pick up a 10mm rice pearl and sew it in the center of the oval, then go through the bead a couple of times. Then follow Steps 9 to 13 of the technique to sew a ring of seed beads around the pearl.

STEP 2

Referring back to the technique, embellish the flowers with the rice pearls, seed beads, and rondelles.

STEP 3

Each of the four flowers should look like this.

STEP 4

Sew 10mm rice pearls and seed bead edges to all the other ovals in the design in the same way as in Step 1. Then add the two crystal montées on the centerline of the design. These montées have four holes, so you sew them on like a four-hole button, going through in a cross shape. When all the beads have been added, cut loosely around the design to remove most of the net.

STEP 5

Pick up the tiara band and shape it using the technique on page 21. Using a fresh piece of thread and a beading needle. Wrap the thread a few times around the tiara band about 3½in (90mm) up from one end. Sew the needle through the wrapped thread to secure it in place.

STEP 6

Place the lace design against the tiara with the end flower sitting on the wrapped thread. Sew through the end petal and back through on the other side of the tiara band. Repeat this stitch again.

STEP 7

Now start moving up the flower, sewing around the tiara band and through the lace, but go under the beads and back down the other side of the tiara band. Keep repeating this stitch wherever you have lace sections sitting on the band. Sew right to the end of the lace and then knot off the thread (see page 23) and cut off any excess. Cut off all the net from around the design edge, taking care not to cut through any stitching when cutting around the lace.

STEP 8

Make up two lace flowers using the technique on pages 68–71, but instead of adding a rondelle and seed bead to the centers, add one 8mm pearl, sewing it so that the hole is running in a horizontal direction. Place one of the lace flowers at the top right of the design and sew it onto the other flowers, attaching it where it sits up against the other flower petals. Sew through all layers to secure the flower. Add the other lace flower at the very bottom of the design, sewing it to the tiara band the same way as you did in Step 6.

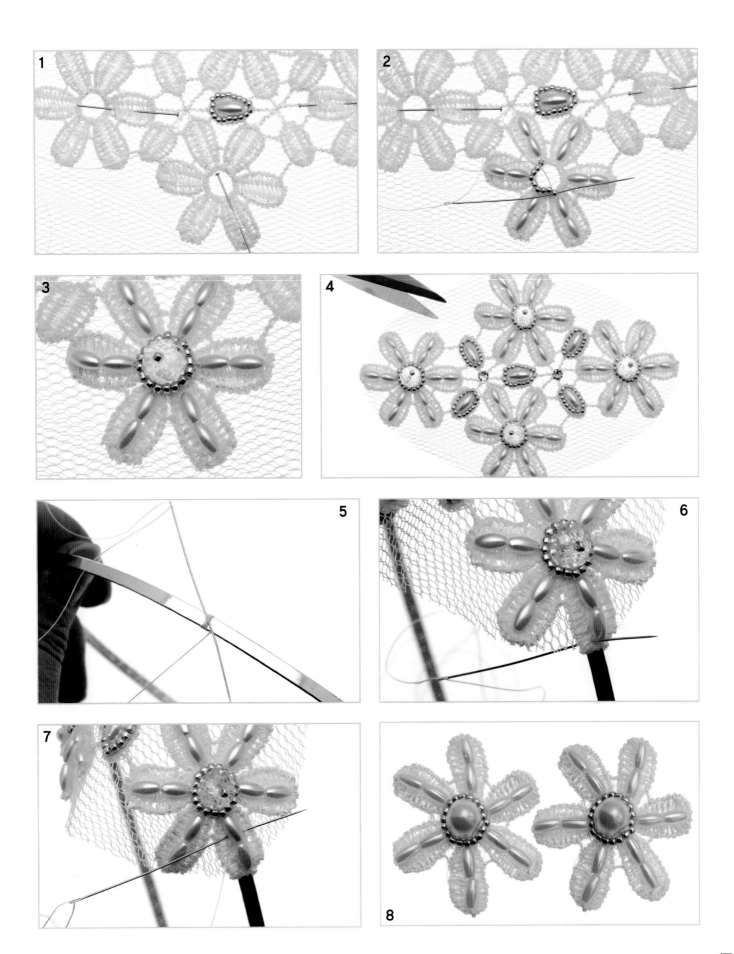

COMB

This comb is embellished with a lace triangle containing two single flowers and a section that has three flowers. The whole piece is glued to a comb, but you can sew it on if you prefer.

You will need

1 x piece of lace with five flowers
Net fabric twice the size of the lace
48 x 3mm by 6mm white rice pearls
1 x 10mm by 4mm white rice pearl
10g x size 11 (1.8mm) silver seed beads
2 x 8mm clear crystal faceted rondelle beads
3 x 8mm white round glass pearls
1 x 4mm crystal montée
Clear plastic comb
Clear adhesive glue
Fine beading thread
Beading needle
Sewing pins
Beading mat
Scissors

STEP 1

Cut out a shape with three flowers and sew around it following Steps 1 to 4 of the technique on pages 68–71. Start in the center of one flower and add an 8mm round pearl. Sew through the pearl, placing the hole horizontal to the lace so that the thread runs through the bead, down each side and through the lace.

STEP 2

Referring back to the technique, follow Steps 9 to 13 to add a seed bead ring around the pearl.

STEP 3

Move your needle and thread across to the central oval piece and repeat Steps 1 and 2 to add the 10mm rice pearl and a seed bead ring to the lace oval. Then bring the needle up to the centre of the design above the oval and add the crystal montée. Montées have four holes and you sew in a cross pattern.

STEP 4

Complete the two other flower centers following Steps 1 and 2.

STEP 5

Make up two single flowers following the technique on pages 68–71.

STEP 6

Working on the flower at the top of the design, add rice pearls to the top three petals, following Steps 5 to 7 of the technique.

STEP 7

Put the two single flowers over the design, placing them in between the top flower and the bottom ones. You should place the flowers so that the central crystal montée still shows. Holding the first flower in place, sew it down by running small stitches along the sides of the rice pearls on the petals.

STEP 8

Add the second single flower and attach in the same way. Allow the flowers to overlap a little as this gives dimension to the design.

STEP 9

Add the rest of the rice pearls to the bottom flowers' petals. You should have the outer three petals showing on each flower and space to add one rice pearl to the top inner petal. The very top petals are covered.

STEP 10

Cut the excess net from around the design, then decide where the comb will sit. Place a fine line of glue along this edge (not where the open net is) and stick the comb down. You may need to prop the comb up while the glue dries so that it doesn't move.

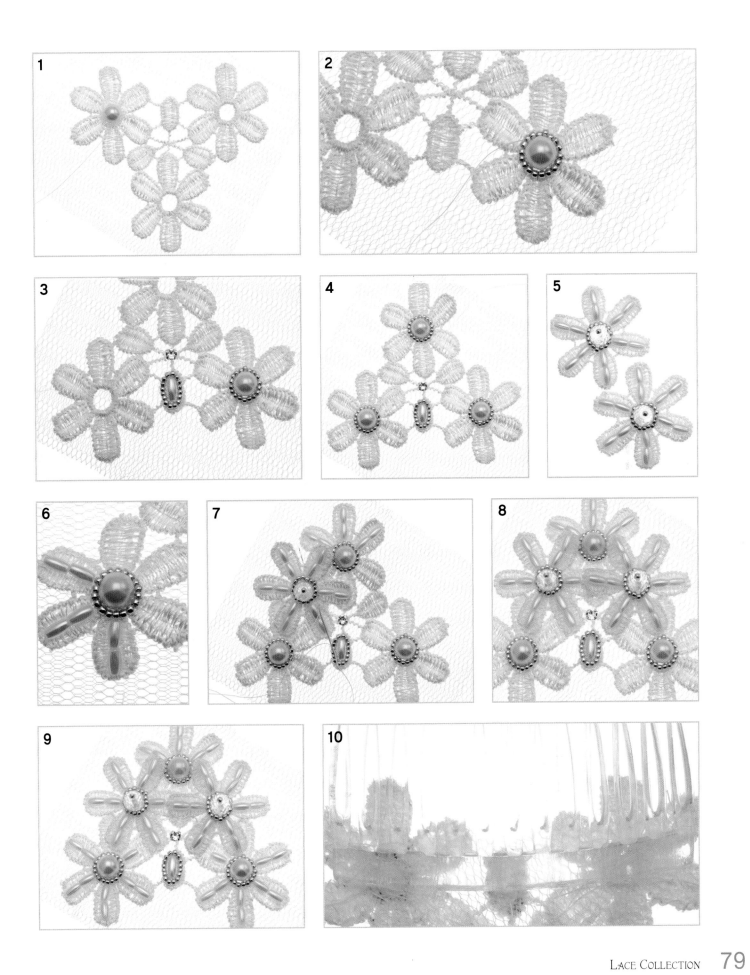

CHOKER

This choker is a simple yet stylish design, using ribbon as the tie that holds it in place comfortably around your neck.

You will need

- 1 x piece of lace with one flower and ovals either side
- 12 x 3mm by 6mm white rice pearls
- 2 x 10mm by 4mm white rice pearls
- 10g x size 11 (1.8mm) silver seed beads
- 1 x 8mm clear crystal faceted rondelle bead
- 40in (1m) x ½in (12mm) wide organza ribbon
- Fine beading thread
- Superglue
- Beading needle
- Sewing pins
- Beading mat
- Scissors

STEP 1

Fold the ribbon in half. Mark the fold with a pin—this is where the middle of the lace will sit.

STEP 2

Cut out a flower with ovals either side and place it on the lace so the design is central. Pin to hold the lace in place.

STEP 3

Thread up a beading needle and sew around the edge of the lace design using small stitches.

STEP 4

When you get to the ribbon edge, sew in a running stitch along the back of the flower, catching as much of the lace pattern as you can. There will be flower petals sticking out on each side; these are fine to leave.

STEP 5

Add a 10mm rice pearl to the center of an oval, sewing through the bead a few times to secure it. Add a ring of seed beads following Steps 9 to 13 of the technique on pages 68–71.

STEP 6

Add the rondelle and a seed bead to the center of the flower following Steps 14 to 15 of the technique.

STEP 7

Add a seed bead ring, following the technique steps again.

STEP 8

Add the 6mm rice pearls to the petals following Steps 5 to 7 of the technique on pages 68–71. Repeat Steps 5 and 6 to complete the final oval. When finished, check you are happy with the length of the ribbon and cut it shorter if you prefer. Place a drop of superglue along the cut edge to seal it.

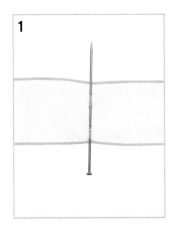

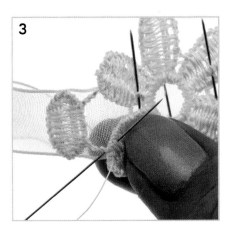

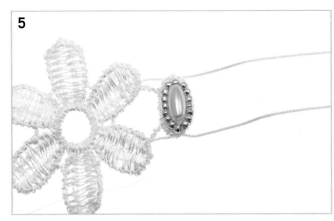

BRACELET

This bracelet has a button and ribbon loop to close it, but you could add lengths of ribbon on both ends and tie the bracelet around the wrist instead.

You will need

1 x piece of lace with three flowers in a row
Net fabric twice the size of the lace
36 x 3mm by 6mm white rice pearls
2 x 10mm by 4mm white rice pearls
10g x size 11 (1.8mm) silver seed beads
4 x 8mm clear crystal faceted rondelle beads
2 x 4mm white round beads
1 x ¾in (18mm) flat pearl button
2in (5cm) x ¼in (6mm) wide white organza ribbon
Fine beading thread
Beading needle
Sewing pins
Beading mat
Scissors

STEP 1

Cut out and sew around the flower shape following Steps 1 to 4 of the technique on pages 68–71. You need to cut a row of 3 flowers, all with an oval on their right.

STEP 2

Referring back to the technique again, add rice pearls to the petals on the first flower. Then start to add the seed bead ring.

STEP 3

Finish the seed bead ring and add the central rondelle.

STEP 4

Move along to the oval next to the flower and add a 10mm rice pearl. It's easiest to work along the design this way as you make best use of the thread, so you are not crossing over yourself or knotting off and starting lots of fresh pieces of thread for each flower and oval. Just keep sewing along until your thread runs short then start with new thread.

STEP 5

Add a seed bead ring to the oval.

STEP 6

Repeat Steps 2 to 5 to complete the other two flowers and one more oval.

STEP 7

Cut around the design to remove all the excess net. Be careful when cutting that you don't cut through any stitches.

STEP 8

To add the button, bring the thread up through the end oval, thread on a 4mm pearl, take the thread through the button from the back and down through the other hole in the button. Thread on another 4mm bead and go through the oval. Then bring the needle back through all the beads and the button to secure. The 4mm beads won't be seen, but help keep the button raised from the lace so the ribbon loop sits tightly underneath the button when the bracelet is worn.

STEP 9

Add a rondelle and seed bead to the top of the button by following Steps 14 and 15 of the technique on pages 68–71.

STEP 10

To add the ribbon loop to the other end, place the end of the ribbon against the back of the end petal and sew along the length of the petal using tiny running stitches. Then attach the other end of the ribbon to the other end petal.

1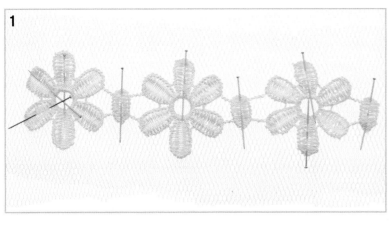

2

3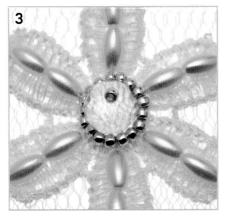

4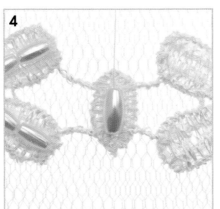

5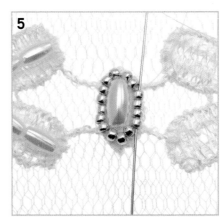

6

7

8

9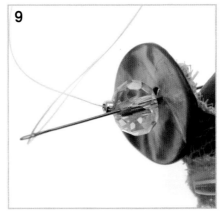

10

BROOCH

This delicate brooch would be great on its own or could be used for a wedding guest to hold her floral buttonhole.

You will need

1 x piece of lace with three flowers in total

Net fabric twice the size of the lace

36 x 3mm by 6mm white rice pearls

2 x 10mm by 4mm white rice pearls

10g x size 11 (1.8mm) silver seed beads

1 x 8mm clear crystal faceted rondelle bead

2 x 8mm white round glass pearls

1 x 4mm crystal montée

1 x 1¼in (30mm) brooch bar

Fine beading thread

Beading needle

Sewing pins

Beading mat

Scissors

STEP 1

Cut out and sew around the flower shape following Steps 1 to 4 of the technique on pages 68–71. You want to cut a row of two flowers with a triangle of ovals in the middle.

STEP 2

Add an 8mm round pearl to the center of a flower. This pearl should have its hole running horizontal—so you cannot see the hole from the top. Go through the pearl a few times to secure it.

STEP 3

Add a seed bead ring around the pearl following Steps 9 to 13 of the technique. Repeat Steps 2 and 3 to add a pearl and seed bead ring to the other flower.

STEP 4

Pick up the montée and sew it to the center of the oval triangle. Go through the holes on the montée in a cross (up and down, then side to side). Referring back to the technique steps, add 10mm rice beads and a seed bead ring to each of the lower ovals.

STEP 5

Make up one single flower following the technique on pages 68–71.

STEP 6

Coming back to the main piece of lace, follow Steps 5 to 7 of the technique to add 6mm rice seeds to the petals on both flowers.

STEP 7

Place the single flower over the center of the design, so that it sits comfortably between the other two flowers. Attach to the base design by using small running stitches alongside the rice pearls on the petals of the single flower.

STEP 8

To attach the brooch bar, bring the needle through to the back and place the bar in the center of the design, about two-thirds of the way up. Go through the hole on the brooch bar with the needle and through the net. Loop around the outside of the brooch bar, bringing the needle through the hole and back around the outside three times on each side of the hole. Move along the bar, doing the same on each hole. Cut off the excess net from around the edge of the design, being careful not to cut into any stitches.

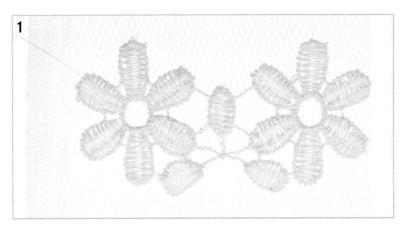

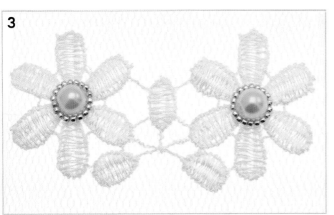

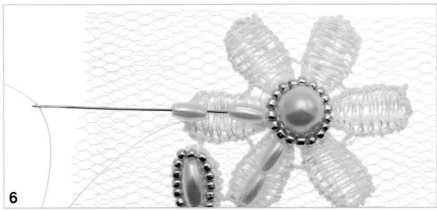

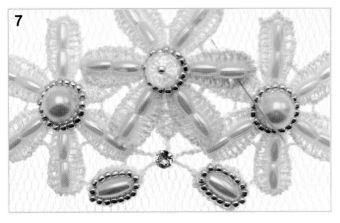

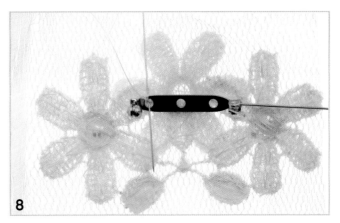

EARRINGS

Making complementary earrings using a lace design can be tricky, but this project shows you it is possible to make lovely little earrings using a tiny part of the lace design.

You will need

1 x piece of lace (with two single ovals)
Net fabric twice the size of the lace
2 x 10mm by 4mm white rice pearls
10g x size 11 (1.8mm) silver seed beads
2 x 4mm flat-pad earring posts
Clear adhesive glue
Sticky tack
Fine beading thread
Beading needle
Sewing pins
Beading mat
Scissors

STEP 1

Cut out two of the oval shapes from the lace.

STEP 2

Back each oval with doubled-up net and pin in place.

STEP 3

Sew around the edge of the lace, taking the beading needle around the lace edge and through the net to hold it together. Add a rice pearl in the center of the oval, then sew through it a few times to secure.

STEP 4

At one end of the pearl, bring the needle through to the front and thread on a seed bead. Go down through the lace the width of the seed bead, away from where the thread exits the lace.

STEP 5

Add another seed bead and go through the lace again the width of the seed bead away from the first bead. Bring the needle back up at the beginning of the seed bead row and go through the two seed beads. Add another bead and go down through the lace and back up at the beginning and through all three beads.

STEP 6

Keep repeating Step 5 to add a complete ring of seed beads around the rice pearl.

STEP 7

Trim off all the excess net as close to the beads as you are comfortable with. Do not cut into the beads as they will fall off.

STEP 8

Add clear adhesive glue to the pad on the earring post and stick it to the back of the earring in the center. Place the earring on a little piece of sticky tack to hold it upside down. Then repeat all the steps to make another earring for a matching pair.

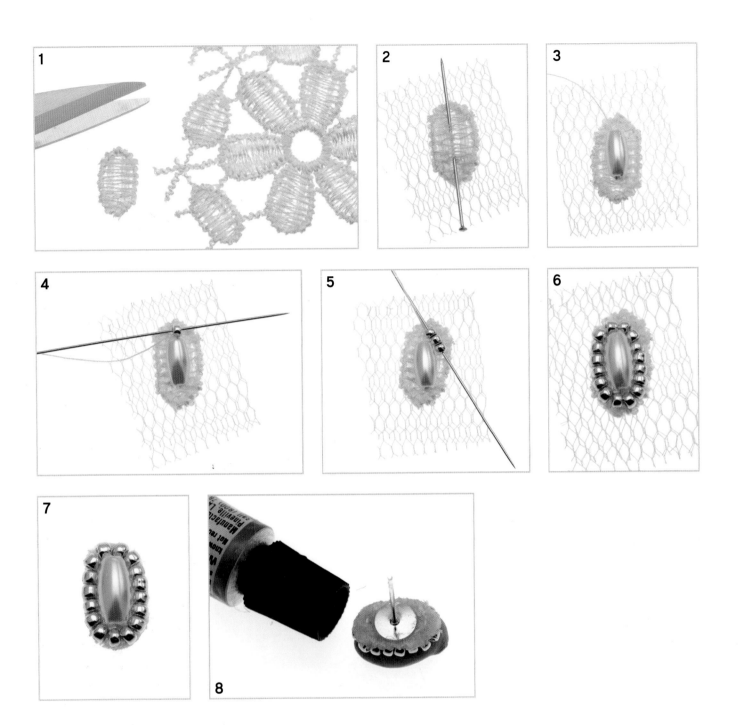

NATURE
Collection

THIS COLLECTION IS DESIGNED AROUND A LEAF-SHAPED charm that comes in a variety of shapes and sizes—just look out for a loop to connect it to the jewelry. Not every bride wants to wear white and have silver accessories, so these pieces have been created in a lovely warm pink tone with rose gold and pale pink pearls. However, the collection would work just as well in silver or gold with white or cream pearls.

FLORAL BRANCH

This technique shows how to create a typical three-flower floral branch using seed beads. In this collection, floral branches are also made using single larger pearls and 4mm pearls and crystals.

You will need

15 x 3.3mm (size 6) seed beads
US 26-gauge (0.4mm) or
    US 24-gauge (0.5mm) wire
Beading mat
Side cutters

These small branches are very adaptable, perfect for use with any wedding design. They can have flowers added easily, so you can create a very ornate branch or make lots of these three-flower ones and add multiples to a tiara for a wild-flower meadow look. Use different-sized beads to make the flowers larger or smaller to vary the style. These kind of flowers look great made with bicone cut faceted crystals too.

STEP 1

Cut a 12in (305mm) length of wire. Thread on five seed beads (or pearls or crystals) and push the beads to the middle of the wire. Bring the wire around into a circle and cross the wires over. This makes a bead flower.

STEP 2

Twist the wires together for just under ¼in (6mm) to make a stem.

STEP 3

Add five more beads to one wire end and push them up to the first bead flower. Just under ¼in (6mm) away from the first flower, cross the wires over.

STEP 4

Twist the two wire ends together until they meet the already twisted stem from the first flower.

STEP 5

Twist the two wires together for about ⅛in (3mm), and then add five more beads onto the piece of wire that is the longest. Bring these beads up to the other flowers, and just under ¼in (6mm) away make them into a circle and cross the wires over.

1

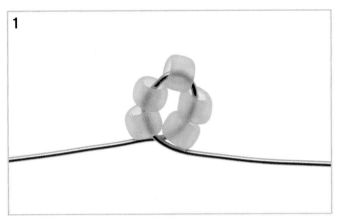

2

3

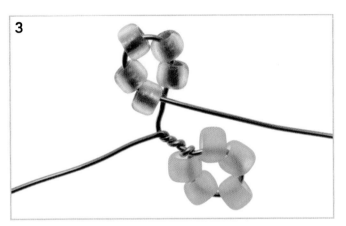

4

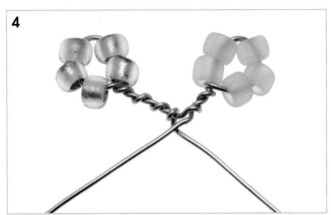

5

6

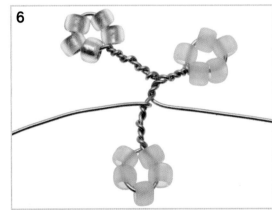

STEP 6

Twist the two wires together until they meet the stem created in Step 5.

STEP 7

Bring the two wire ends together and twist for just under ¼in (6mm). This completes the floral branch.

7

PEARL FLOWER

Pearl flowers feature many times in this collection. You can make them with any beads and pearls. Always use a larger size of bead for the center of the flower.

You will need

5 x 4mm glass pearls
1 x 6mm glass pearl
US 26-gauge (0.4mm) or
US 24-gauge (0.5mm) wire
Beading mat
Side cutters

STEP 1

Cut an 8in (200mm) length of wire. This will be far too much wire but makes it much easier to handle the flower. Thread on the five 4mm pearls and wrap the wire around into a circle so the wires cross over and all the pearls sit closely together.

STEP 2

Twist the wire ends together twice and bend the twist so that it sits at a right angle to the beads.

STEP 3

Bring one end of the wire through the center of the pearls.

STEP 4

Add a 6mm pearl to this wire and pull it back through the center until the 6mm pearl sits tight up against the pearl ring.

STEP 5

On the back bring the wires together and twist.

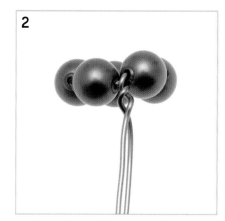

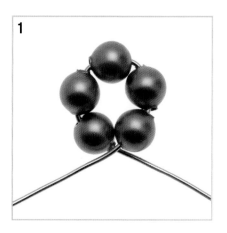

SIDE TIARA

A gorgeous piece for a wedding, this is made up of floral branches wrapped around a tiara and pearl flowers. The tiara has a gold or silver tiara band, as rose gold bands are not currently available to purchase. On most tiaras the band doesn't show, so it shouldn't matter if the color does not quite match the decoration.

You will need

8 x ¾in (20mm) rose gold-colored leaves with hanging loop
1 x roll of US 24-gauge (0.5mm) rose gold-colored copper wire
48 x 3mm pale pink glass pearls
20 x 4mm powder almond glass pearls
3 x 6mm pale pink glass pearls
40 x 2.5mm (size 8) frosted pale pink seed beads
30 x 2.5mm (size 8) shiny pale pink seed beads
1 x silver or gold-colored tiara band
Superglue
Beading mat
Chain-nose pliers
Round-nose pliers
Side cutters

STEP 1

Make eight floral branches (see pages 92–3), four using only 3mm pink pearls and the other four using a combination of seed beads. Make two branches with two pink five-bead seed bead flowers and one frosted flower in the middle. Make two more branches reversed, so they have two frosted flowers with a central pink flower. Add each branch to a leaf and wrap the wire ends around the base of the leaf above the loop. Add a 4mm pearl on one wire end and push both wire ends through the loop on the leaf.

STEP 2

On all eight leaf floral branches, pull the 4mm pearl tight against the loop on the leaf and twist the wire ends together below the leaf for about 1in (25mm).

STEP 3

Pick up the tiara band and manipulate it into a comfortable shape (see page 21). Start to add the leaf floral branches to the tiara band. This is a side tiara design so should sit to one side of the band. Work from the center of the band down toward one end. To wrap a branch, place the branch against the side of the tiara band with the wire ends either side of the band. Wrap both wire ends around the band a few times. Leave the ends on for the moment. Add another branch facing in the opposite direction and wrap around the tiara band.

STEP 4

Add another four branches so you have three on each side of the band. Wrap them so that they sit evenly on the band. Add the final two branches, one on each end. This time place them centrally on the tiara band, not to one side. Check the placement of all the branches and that they are secure. When you are happy with the arrangement, cut off all the excess wire ends.

STEP 5

Use the chain-nose pliers to make sure all the ends are sitting flat against the tiara band.

STEP 6

Take the round-nose pliers and add a curve into all the twisted wire stems. This will bring them in toward each other more.

STEP 7

Work with the arrangement until you are happy with the way it looks.

STEP 8

Make three pearl flowers (see pages 94–5); two flowers should have a 6mm pink pearl center and 4mm powder almond pearls around the edge. The other flower has 10 frosted pink seed beads around the edge and a 6mm powder almond pearl in the middle. Wire-wrap these to the tiara band inside the design, so they sit in the middle. The two matching flowers go at either end with the seed bead flower in the center.

STEP 9

Make a floral branch (see pages 92–3) with two seed bead flowers and three single pearls.

STEP 10

Add the floral branch next to the seed bead flower. Make curves in all the twisted stems on the pearl flowers. Have a final play with the arrangement before cutting off any excess wire ends. To finish, make sure all wire ends are tucked in tightly against the tiara band so they don't snag your hair. Run your fingers over the inside of the tiara band and add superglue to any wires that still feel a bit sharp.

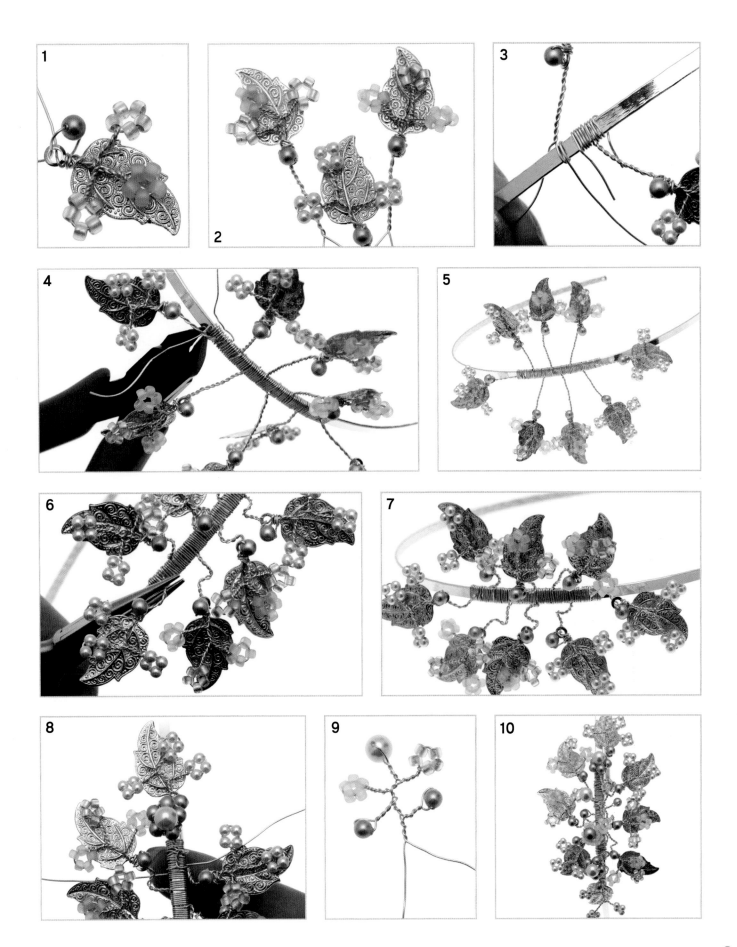

HAIRPIN

A combination of leaves and pearl flowers make up an elegant and intricate hairpin. Perfect as a set of three pins, these also look great on their own.

You will need

- 3 x ¾in (20mm) rose gold-colored leaves with hanging loop
- 1 x roll of US 24-gauge (0.5mm) rose gold-colored copper wire
- 24 x 3mm pale pink glass pearls
- 16 x 4mm powder almond glass pearls
- 3 x 6mm pale pink glass pearls
- 15 x 3.3mm (size 6) frosted pale pink seed beads
- 1 x large hairpin
- Superglue
- Beading mat
- Chain-nose pliers
- Round-nose pliers
- Side cutters

STEP 1

Make up three floral branches following the technique on pages 92–3. Two of the branches use 3mm pink pearls. The other branch uses frosted seed beads. Take a leaf and place a branch with the wire ends either side of the loop on the leaf. Wrap the wire around the base of the leaf just above the loop, so each wire end goes around the leaf once from different directions. You should end up with a wire on either side of each leaf. Make up all three pieces in this way. If the leaves you are using have a direction like these ones, make sure the pearl branch pieces have the leaves facing the opposite way to each other.

STEP 2

Using the pearl flower technique (see pages 94–5), make three flowers using 4mm powder almond pearls for the outside and a 6mm pink pearl for the center. Twist the wire on two of the flowers to make stalks that are about 1in (25mm) long. On the third flower, finish with the wires facing in opposite directions.

STEP 3

Pick up the leaf piece with the seed bead branch and thread a 4mm pearl onto one of the wires. Bring the wire around the loop and place the pearl so it sits on top of the loop.

STEP 4

On the back of the leaf, twist the wire with the pearl together with the other wire. Make sure as you twist them together that the pearl is sitting right in the middle of the loop on the front. Twist until the section is about 1¼in (32mm) long.

STEP 5

Hold the leaf piece in your hand and add a pearl flower with a twisted stalk either side of it. All three pieces have two wires below the twisted section. Holding onto one wire from each piece, place the hairpin against the wires and wrap all three wires on one side of the pin and the other wire ends on the opposite side. This is tricky and a bit fiddly so be patient. Make sure the pieces are sitting centrally on the top of the pin.

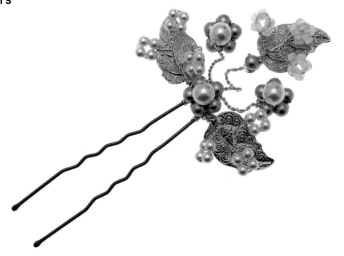

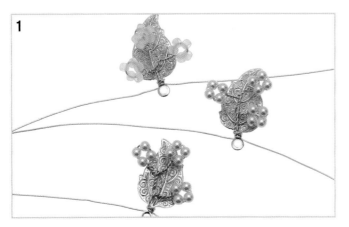

1

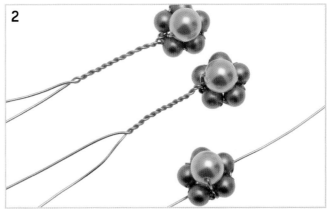

2

3

4

5

STEP 6

Wrap the other three wire ends around the opposite side of the hairpin and then cut off all the excess wire ends using the side cutters. Using chain-nose pliers, push all the ends against the pin so they sit flat.

STEP 7

Using round-nose pliers, create spirals in the stems. Arrange the pieces so that the leaf sits in the middle, above the pearl flowers.

6

7

STEP 8

Pick up both of the leaf pieces with the pearl floral branches. Thread both wire ends through the middle of the loop from the front.

STEP 9

Add a leaf piece to the side of the hairpin. Place the loop on top of the wire coil and wrap one wire end below it. It should sit next to the pearl flower. If the leaf has a direction, then have it so the point on the end of the leaf is facing up.

STEP 10

Wrap the other wire end above the loop on the leaf, wrapping over the wire coil that is already there. Stop wrapping when you get to the twisted wire stems.

STEP 11

Add the other leaf piece on the opposite side, making sure the leaf is also facing up. When both leaves are secure, cut off any excess wire and push the ends against the pin.

STEP 12

Take the pearl flower (which you made in Step 2) that has the wires facing in opposite directions and place it over the center of the hairpin so that it covers up all the wrapped wire. Bring both wire ends on this flower around to the back of the hairpin with one end going through the middle of the hairpin and the other between the top leaf piece and one of the pearl flowers.

STEP 13

On the back of the hairpin twist the two wire ends together for about 1in (25mm). Check the front of the hairpin to make sure the pearl flower hasn't moved and is still central to the design.

STEP 14

Cut off the excess wire beyond the twisted section and curl the twist into a circle using round-nose pliers. Place this circle against the back of the hairpin.

STEP 15

Finally, add a little superglue to hold the curled wire in place. This will also help the wire to not pull on your hair when worn.

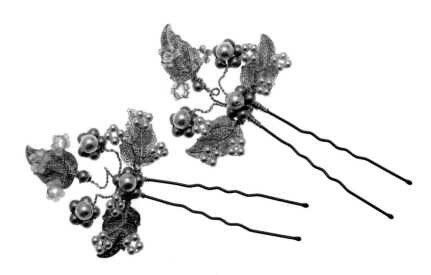

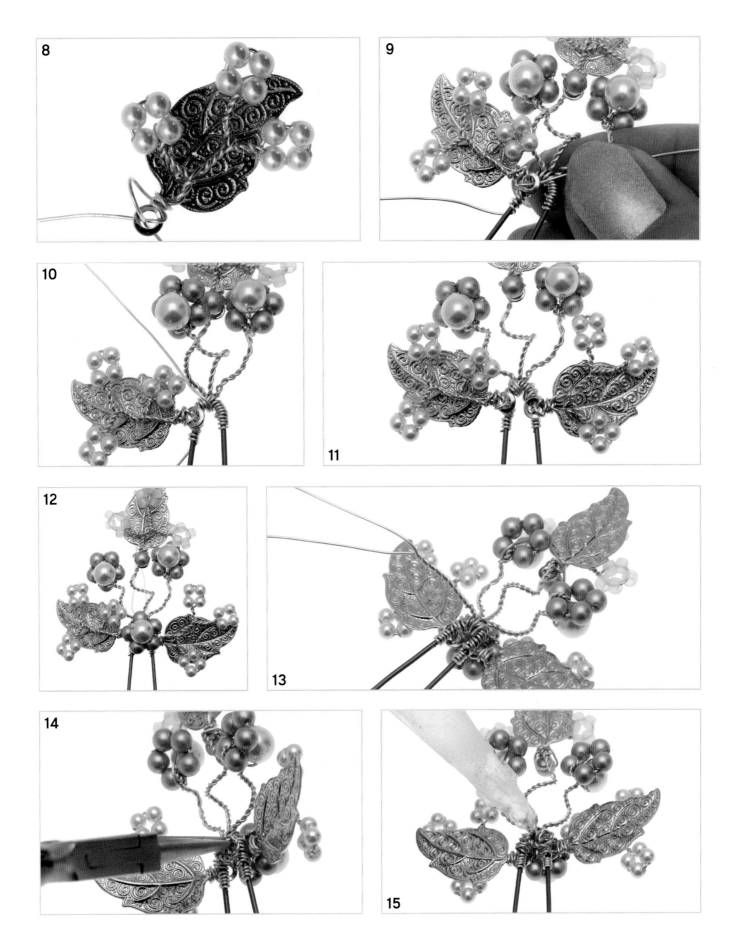

NECKLACE

This delicate necklace of leaves, crystal beads, and pearls curves gracefully around the nape of the neck.

You will need

- 3 x ¾in (20mm) rose gold-colored leaves with hanging loop
- 1 x roll of US 20-gauge (0.8mm) rose gold-colored copper wire
- 1 x roll of US 26-gauge (0.4mm) rose gold-colored copper wire
- 6 x rose gold-colored calottes
- 1 x rose gold-colored lobster clasp
- 1 x 4mm, 1 x 6mm rose gold-colored jumpring
- 1 x roll of white beading cord
- 12 x 3mm, 2 x 6mm pale pink glass pearls
- 2 x 4mm, 4 x 6mm powder almond glass pearls
- 28 x 4mm pale pink crystal bicones
- 44 x 2.5mm (size 8) frosted pale pink seed beads
- 46 x 2.5mm (size 8) shiny pale pink seed beads
- Beading mat
- Chain-nose pliers
- Round-nose pliers
- Side cutters
- Superglue

STEP 1

This necklace naturally sits on the neck by the collarbones. To make it longer you need to add extra length to the wires, making sure one wire is ¾in (20mm) longer than the other. Cut two pieces of US 20-gauge (0.8mm) wire, one 6¼in (160mm) long and the other 7in (180mm) long. Make simple loops at the ends of both wires (see pages 26–7). This wire will have a natural curve as it comes on a roll, so allow it to stay in that shape as it will sit nicely around the neck.

STEP 2

Cut about 12in (305mm) of US 26-gauge (0.4mm) wire and wrap it around the outside curved wire six times. Thread on a 4mm crystal and wrap around the inner wire six times.

Add a crystal and wrap around the outer wire again. Repeat this to add five crystals in total.

STEP 3

After the fifth crystal, coil the wire around the inner curved wire six times and then add a leaf, bring the wire through the loop and wrap around the base of the leaf twice. Wrap tightly to the inner curved wire. Finish with the wire sitting by the side of the leaf loop.

STEP 4

Add a 4mm powder almond pearl to the wire and wrap over the top of the loop so that the pearl sits on the loop. Now coil the wire six times around the inner curved wire underneath the leaf. Cut off any excess wire using side cutters.

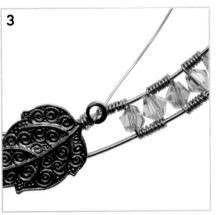

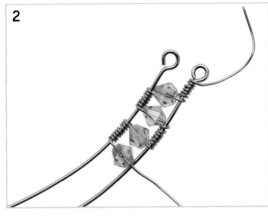

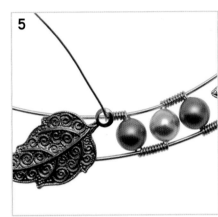

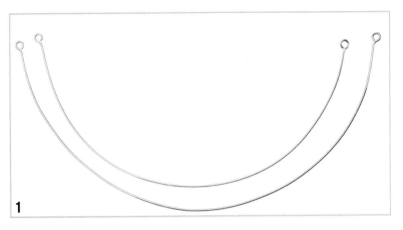

STEP 5

Start with a fresh piece of US
26-gauge (0.4mm) wire and coil it
around the outer wire for about ½in
(13mm). Add a 6mm powder almond
pearl and coil the wire around the
inner curved wire eight times. Add
a 6mm pink pearl and coil the wire
around the outer curved wire eight
times. Add a final 6mm powder almond
pearl and coil the wire around the
inner curved wire another six times.
Add a leaf to the wire.

STEP 6

At this point you should be at the
center of the curved wire shape.
If not, maneuver the pieces until the
leaf you have just added is sitting
at the central point. Wrap the leaf
to the inner wire twice around the
base of the leaf between the loop
and the leaf. Bring the wire down
behind the leaf and coil the wire
around the outer curved wire a few
times. Picture 6 shows a view of the
necklace from the back.

STEP 7

Add three more 6mm pearls the same way as in Step 5. Finish with the wire coiled eight times around the inner curved wire. Cut off any excess wire.

STEP 8

Cut a new piece of US 26-gauge (0.4mm) wire and coil around the inner curved wire six times. Add a leaf and place it so that it mirrors the one on the opposite side of the necklace. Coil the wire around the base of the leaf to secure it. Picture 8 shows the back view.

STEP 9

Add a 4mm powder almond pearl to the wire and place it over the leaf loop. Wrap around the inner wire. Coil the wire a few times and add five 4mm crystals, repeating the pattern from Step 2. If you run out of room to add all the crystals, gently push the design down the curved wires to make extra space.

STEP 10

Make three floral branches (see pages 92–3). They should have two, three-crystal flowers with four beads (3mm pearls) in the middle.

STEP 11

Add the floral branches on the necklace piece, wrapping them next to the leaves. On the two side leaves the branch goes on the outer curved wire and on the central leaf the branch sits on the inner curved wire.

STEP 12

When you have added the floral branches the whole design should look like this.

STEP 13

Cut four pieces of beading cord 8in (200mm) long. Attach each piece to a calotte (see page 20). Thread 23 shiny and 22 frosted seed beads alternately onto each cord.

STEP 14

Hold two cords together and push both through the hole in a calotte. This can be tricky, so add a tiny drop of superglue to the cord ends to make them stiff, as that will help.

STEP 15

Knot the cords and close the calottes.

STEP 16

Add a calotte to each loop on the necklace.

STEP 17

On the ends of the beading, add a 6mm jumpring (see page 18) to one side and the lobster clasp to the other side using the 4mm jumpring. Make sure both jumprings are properly closed to finish.

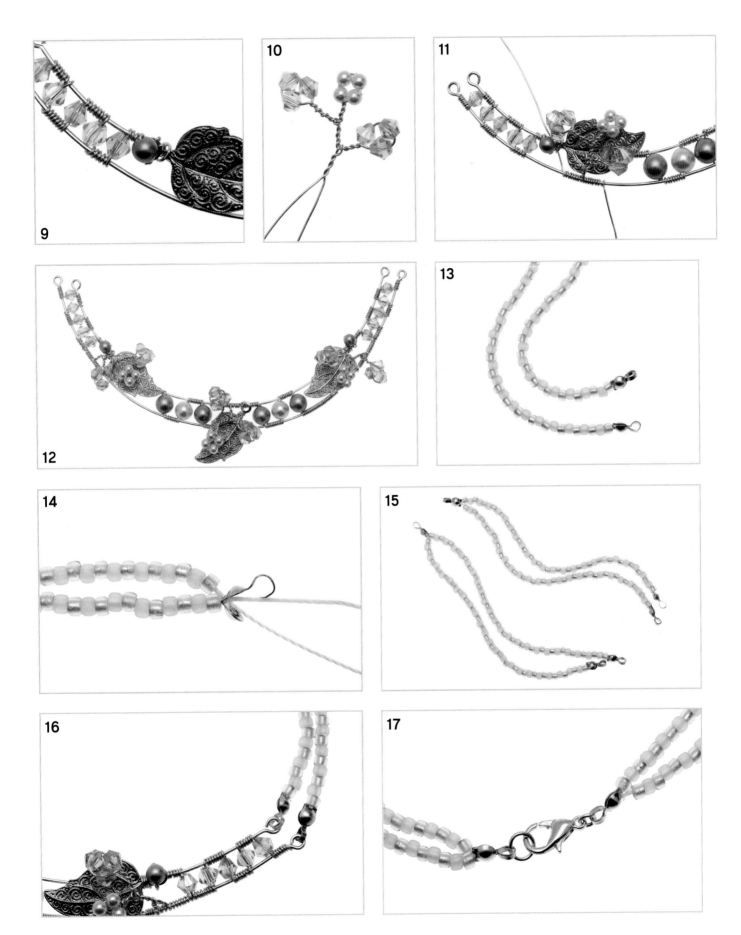

BRACELET

This elegant bracelet with its pretty leaves, pearls, and bicones is made to suit the size of your wrist. Choose any leaf charm that has a loop to complete this bangle-style bracelet.

You will need

4 x ¾in (20mm) rose gold-colored leaves with hanging loop
1 x roll of US 20-gauge (0.8mm) rose gold-colored copper wire
1 x roll of US 26-gauge (0.4mm) rose gold-colored copper wire
1 x rose gold-colored three-loop magnetic barrel clasp
8 x 6mm pale pink glass pearls
8 x 6mm powder almond glass pearls
15 x 4mm pale pink crystal bicones
Beading mat
Superglue
Masking tape
Chain-nose pliers
Round-nose pliers
Side cutters

STEP 1

Measure your wrist and add ¾in (20mm). Cut three pieces of US 20-gauge (0.8mm) wire to this length. As the wire comes on a roll, the wire will naturally make a round shape so when you cut the wire try not to disturb this shape too much. Make a "P"-shape loop on the ends of all the wires using round-nose pliers. To do this, grasp the very end of the wire in the pliers and curl around until it meets the wire. When you have all the loops made, manipulate the wires into a matching oval shape. Make sure all three wires match each other. When you are happy that they do, open the loops on one end (the same end on all the wires) by twisting the loop to one side (see page 18). Thread the loop onto one side of the three-loop clasp and close the loop. Add the next wire. When you have added all three loops on one side, repeat for the other half of the clasp.

STEP 2

Before adding any beads, think about the shape of the bracelet. Try it on and make sure it feels comfortable. Next add a couple of pieces of masking tape to hold the wires apart from each other. This will make it easier to add beads.

STEP 3

Cut a 12in (305mm) length of US 26-gauge (0.4mm) wire and thread on two pink and two powder almond 6mm pearls. Push them to the middle of the wire and form them into a square, then twist the wire ends together twice. Bend the twist so it's at a right angle to the beads.

STEP 4

Bring one wire end through the middle of the pearl square and add a 4mm crystal. Bring the wire end back through the middle again and pull tight. This will trap the crystal on one side of the pearls. Bend the wire end so it's facing the opposite way to the other wire end.

STEP 5

Start in the middle of the bracelet, at the opposite side to the clasp. Place the four-pearl square across all three wires and wrap the wire ends around the outer bracelet wires five times.

STEP 6

Add a leaf to the wrapping wire and coil twice around the base of the leaf to secure.

STEP 7

Loosely coil the wire behind the leaf about halfway along the leaf. Bring the wrapping wire to the middle bracelet wire, coil once and add a 6mm pearl. Coil the wrapping wire six times around the outer bracelet wire.

STEP 8

Add a 6mm pearl and bring the wrapping wire back to the middle bracelet wire. Coil once and add a leaf, wrap twice around the base of the leaf. Then coil a couple of times around the wire behind the leaf and cut off any excess with side cutters.

STEP 9

Cut a new 12in (305mm) piece of US 26-gauge (0.4mm) wire and coil a few times under the same leaf. Add a 6mm pearl and coil eight times around the outer wire. Add another 6mm pearl and bring the wrapping wire back to the middle bracelet wire.

STEP 10

Coil six times and add a 6mm pearl. Bring the wire across to the opposite outer wire and wrap eight times. Add a final 6mm pearl. Coil the wrapping wire around the middle bracelet wire eight times and add a row of five 4mm crystals, wrapping five times in between each one. Cut off any excess wire.

STEP 11

Cut a new 12in (305mm) piece of US 26-gauge (0.4mm) wire and coil on the middle bracelet wire from the 6mm pearls to the square pearl shape in the center of the bracelet. When you get to the square, bring the wrapping wire across to the back of the leaf, add a 4mm crystal and wrap once over the loop on the leaf so that the crystal sits on the loop. Bring the wrapping wire across the back again and add another crystal to the other leaf loop.

STEP 12

Go back to Step 6 and repeat the rest of the steps for the other side of the bracelet. Follow the step exactly as you don't want a mirror repeat. Finally, add a little glue to any wire ends that feel rough to the touch and could scratch the skin when wearing the bracelet.

1

2

3

4

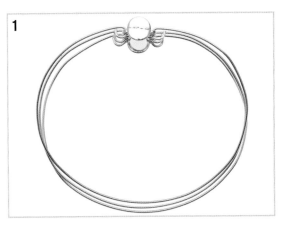

5

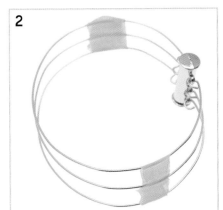

6

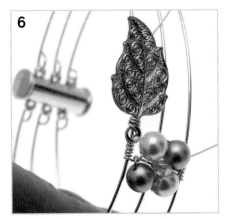

7

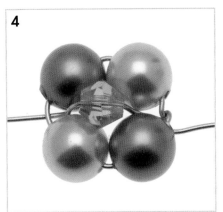

8

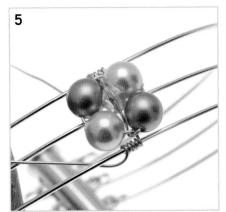

9

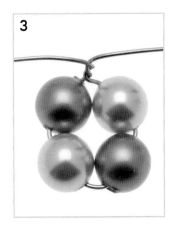

10

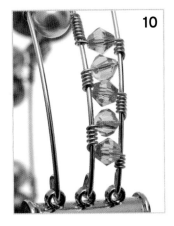

11

12

EARRINGS

These delightful earrings would be a great addition to any outfit. For a shorter style, simply leave out the beaded eyepins made in Step 1 and attach the drop and charm to the earwire.

You will need

- 2 x ¾in (20mm) rose gold-colored leaves with hanging loop
- 2 x 2in (50mm) rose gold-colored eyepins
- 2 x 1in (25mm) rose gold-colored headpins
- 2 x 2mm rose gold-colored metal beads
- 4 x 4mm rose gold-colored metal beads
- 2 x 3mm pale pink glass pearls
- 2 x 4mm powder almond glass pearls
- 2 x 6mm powder almond glass pearls
- 2 x 4mm pale pink crystal bicones
- 2 x rose gold-colored earwires
- Beading mat
- Chain-nose pliers
- Round-nose pliers
- Side cutters

STEP 1

Take the two eyepins and thread on a 4mm pearl, 4mm metal bead, 4mm crystal, and 3mm pearl. Make simple loops (see pages 26–7) at the ends on both eyepins.

STEP 2

Make two beaded dangles on the headpins. On each pin place a 2mm metal bead, a 6mm pearl, and a 4mm metal bead. Make simple loops at the ends on both headpins.

STEP 3

Open the loop on a beaded eyepin by the 3mm pearl. Don't pull the loop outward, but twist gently to one side to open the loop. If you pull it straight out, the shape will distort. Add a beaded dangle and a leaf shape to the loop then close it. Make sure the loop is tightly closed. Repeat this for the other eyepin.

STEP 4

Open the loop on the opposite end of the eyepin, add an earwire, then close the loop. When making the second earring check that the leaf shapes mirror each other rather than facing in the same direction.

1

2

3

4

The earrings shown here are a simple and elegant statement. You could create a cluster effect and make these earrings bolder by adding a jumpring to the eyepin in Step 3. That would allow you more room to add extra beaded drops and leaf charms to the bottom of the earrings.

PENDANT

A filigree rose gold-colored leaf creates the center of this pendant necklace, decorated with four hanging leaves, pearls, and crystals.

You will need

4 x ¾in (20mm) rose gold-colored leaves with hanging loop
1 x 1¾in (45mm) rose gold-colored filigree leaf with 8 loops
2 x 3mm, 2 x 6mm pale pink glass pearls
6 x 4mm, 1 x 6mm powder almond glass pearls
6 x 4mm pink crystal bicones
1 x 2mm, 3 x 4mm rose gold-colored metal beads
10g x 2.5mm (size 8) frosted pale pink seed beads
10g x 2.5mm (size 8) shiny pale pink seed beads
2 x 2in (50mm) rose gold-colored eyepins
7 x 2in (50mm) rose gold-colored headpins
4 x rose gold-colored crimp beads
4 x 3mm rose gold-colored crimp covers
11 x 4mm, 2 x 6mm, 1 x 8mm rose gold-colored jumprings
1 x rose gold-colored lobster clasp
1 x roll of white beading cord
Beading mat
Chain-nose pliers
Round-nose pliers
Side cutters

STEP 1

Take two 4mm jumprings, open them (see page 18), and attach two leaves to loops on either side of the filigree leaf. Add another leaf in the center with the large 8mm jumpring.

STEP 2

Make up five beaded headpins. Two pins have 4mm crystals and 4mm rose gold beads. Two pins have 6mm pink pearls and 4mm rose gold beads. The other pin has a 2mm rose gold bead, 6mm powder almond pearl, and a 4mm rose gold bead. All the pins are finished with a wrapped loop (see pages 18–19).

STEP 3

Make two further beaded headpins, each with a frosted pink seed bead, 4mm powder almond pearl, 3mm pink pearl, 4mm powder almond pearl, and another frosted seed bead. Make wrapped loops at the top.

STEP 4

Make up two beaded eyepins. Thread onto each eyepin a frosted pink seed bead, 4mm crystal, 4mm powder almond pearl, 4mm crystal, and a frosted pink seed bead. Make simple loops (see pages 26–7) at the open ends.

STEP 5

Cut two 12in (300mm) pieces of beading cord. Take a crimp bead and thread onto one piece, add a 4mm jumpring, take the thread back through the crimp bead and pull the thread tight against the jumpring. Close the crimp (see page 22) and add a crimp cover. Repeat this on the other piece of cord.

STEP 6

Thread frosted and shiny pink seed beads alternately onto the crimped thread until each beaded cord is 10in (250mm) long. Add crimp beads to the ends and the beaded eyepins, then take the cords back through the crimp beads and pull tight. Close the crimps and add covers. Open the loops on the other end of the eyepins and attach to the top of the filigree leaf.

STEP 7

On the necklace ends add a 6mm jumpring to one side and the clasp to the other using a 4mm jumpring (see page 18).

STEP 8

Take a 6mm jumpring and the final leaf and the beaded headpin with the powder almond pearl. Thread the jumpring through the same loop as the eyepins and thread on the leaf first and then the headpin. Close the jumpring. Make sure the leaf and beaded headpin sit facing forward.

STEP 9

To finish, take the rest of the 4mm jumprings and attach the other beaded headpins to the bottom loops on the filigree leaf. Use the smallest ones with the 4mm crystals on the top loops. Add the 6mm pink pearl pins to the loop below the side leaves, then add the long thin beaded pins to either side of the middle leaf.

1

2

3

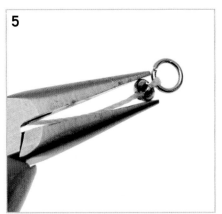

4

5

6

7

8

9

FLORAL
Collection

FLORAL ACCESSORIZING PROVIDES A LOVELY FEMININE touch for brides who prefer a more minimal look. There are two ways to make the versatile flowers in this collection: either with the crystals threaded onto the wire to make a crystal edge with an open petal, or with the crystals wired into the center of each petal to make a filled flower. Pink has been chosen for the filled flowers, but you can match the crystal color to the outfits to be worn.

WIRE FLOWER

The first of two techniques—this version of the wire flower is plain and the crystal decoration is added in the project steps. This wire flower is very versatile as you can create either small flowers or much bigger ones. If creating very small flowers use a finer wire—and if making flowers over 6in (150mm), then you need a thicker wire.

You will need

1 x roll of US 20-gauge
(0.8mm) wire
1 x roll of US 26-gauge
(0.4mm) wire
Beading mat
Masking tape
Chain-nose pliers, side cutters
Tape measure

STEP 1

Take the roll of US 20-gauge (0.8mm) wire and cut off the two ends holding the wire tight. Release the wire and allow the coil to settle to its natural size. The wire should be about 3½in (90mm) across. Step 1 of the specific project will tell you how many coils you need to cut. (The step images in this example use three coils.)

STEP 2

Cut coils from the pack of wire using side cutters and about 3¼in (80mm) from one end. Using chain-nose pliers bend the wire into a right angle facing away from the rest of the coil.

STEP 3

Cut off half a coil from the roll and in the middle of this piece grasp the wire with chain-nose pliers and bend

in half until it resembles a thin petal. This petal shape needs to be the size dictated in the project. This is your petal template.

STEP 4

Take the coils cut in step 2; start from the end that has the right-angle bend. Make a petal shape by laying the wire over the petal template; using chain-nose pliers bend the wire in the same place so it matches the template.

STEP 5

Keep bending the wire until you have five matching petal shapes. On the final petal, bend the wire down to match the right angle on the first petal.

STEP 6

Hold the two right-angle wires together and use a small piece of masking tape to hold them in place. Place the tape about 2in (50mm) down the wires so it's out of the way.

STEP 7

Cut a length of about 12in (305mm) of US 26-gauge (0.4mm) wire and wrap it around the two taped wires. Start about ¼in (6mm) away from the flower and wrap toward the petals.

STEP 8

Bring the US 26-gauge (0.4mm) wire up between two petals and wrap over the top of one petal. Pull the wire tight so the petal closes up and then wrap over the next petal. Pull the wire tight again and repeat wrapping under and over the petals to close them all.

STEP 9

Go around the flower once more wrapping over the petals that you previously wrapped under. When you have finished this step you should have wire wrapped over and under each petal. The petals should be sitting as close to each other as possible. Leave the wire end free.

STEP 10

To shape the petals, pull gently outward with your fingers. This will make the petals open up. The finished shape is up to you, but try to make sure all the petals are the same shape.

STEP 11

When you have shaped the petals the flower is ready for the project.

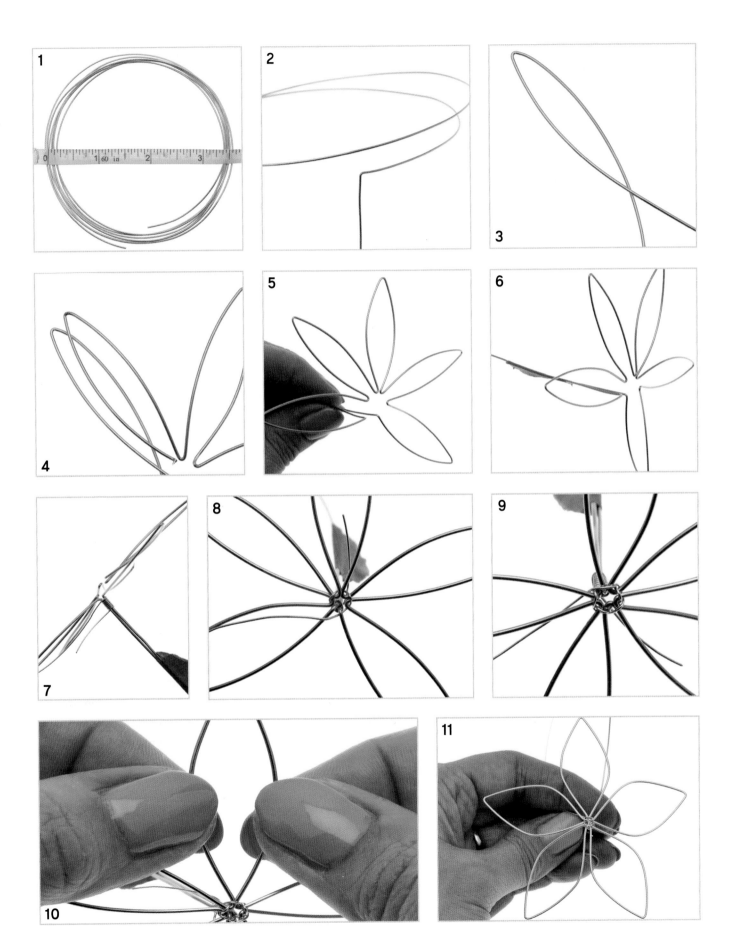

CRYSTAL-EDGE FLOWER

This second technique shows the version that has crystals and seed beads threaded onto the wire. These flowers have petals with an open center. Both techniques use the same basic way of making the flower shape. The quantity of crystals needed is specified in each project.

You will need

1 x roll of US 20-gauge
(0.8mm) wire
1 x roll of US 26-gauge
(0.4mm) wire
4mm crystal bicones
1.8mm (size 11) seed beads
Beading mat
Masking tape
Chain-nose pliers
Side cutters

STEP 1

Follow Steps 1 and 2 of the wire flower technique (see pages 120–21) to start. Thread seed beads and crystals (use the quantity the project specifies) onto the coiled end of the wire, starting with a seed bead, and push them all the way along to sit up against the right-angle bend you have created. Using chain-nose pliers bend the end of the wire as close as possible to the last bead and back down toward the beaded section. The trick with these flowers is to work with the natural curve that the coiled wire already has as this naturally creates the petal shape.

STEP 2

Add more seed beads and crystals, always starting with a seed bead. Alternating the seed beads and crystals will help the petal sit comfortably at the petal points. Take the chain-nose pliers and bend the end of the wire as close to the last crystal as possible. Bend gently as the crystals are made of glass so can crack very easily. Bend the wire back toward the first petal you have created so the wire makes a "V" shape.

STEP 3

Make a second petal using Steps 3 and 4. Remember to always start with a seed bead. Bend the wire end into the "V" shape. This makes the second petal.

STEP 4

You can now see how the flower is starting to form. Repeat the steps to make three more petals. You need five in total. When you have added the beads to the last petal, bend the wire down to match the angle of the wire on the opposite end.

STEP 5

Bring the two wire ends together and place a little masking tape around both wires to hold them in place. Cut about 20in (500mm) of US 26-gauge (0.4mm) wire and wrap around the two wires starting about ¼in (6mm) from the flower. Wrap toward the flower.

STEP 6

Bring the wire between two petals and wrap over the top of one petal. Push the wire down between this petal and the next one along. You want the wire to sit as tight into the corner of the petal as possible. Pull the wire tight; this will close up the petal that the wire crosses.

STEP 7

Wrap the wire under the next petal along and pull tight to close this up.

STEP 8

Continue to weave the wire across the top of the next petal and under the next. Pull as you go; you need the petals to close up so you end up with a gap of about ¼in (6mm) in the very center with all the petals closed.

1

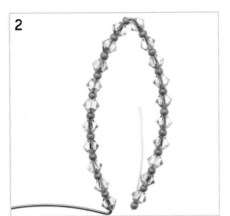

2

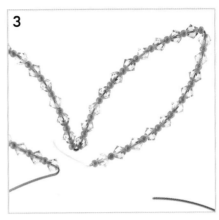

3

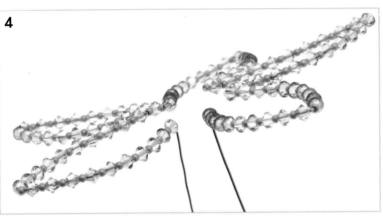

4

5

STEP 9

When you have wrapped the wire all the way around, reverse direction and go back, wrapping over the petals you have already wrapped under. Wrap under all the petals that have wire wrapped over them. When you finish, you should have one piece of wire on each side of every petal. Finish with the wire facing the top of the flower. You are now ready to start the project.

6

7

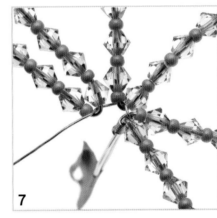

8

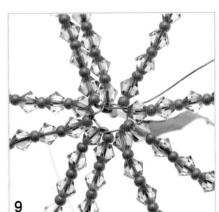

9

WIRE FLOWER SIDE TIARA

Filled with gorgeous colored bicones, this flower is about 5½in (140mm) wide and makes a stunning headpiece.

You will need

1 x roll of US 20-gauge (0.8mm) gold-colored wire

1 x roll of US 26-gauge (0.4mm) gold-colored wire

250 x 4mm colored (of your choice) crystal bicones

10g x 1.8mm (size 11) gold seed beads

1 x gold-colored tiara band

Beading mat

Superglue

Masking tape

Chain-nose pliers

Side cutters

Tape measure

STEP 1

Make a wire flower by following the technique on pages 120–21. You need to cut a length of three coils for this flower. The petal template needs to be 3in (75mm) long. Bring the US 26-gauge (0.4mm) wire between two petals and wrap the wire around the flower stem wires six or more times so the flower is securely tied together. Cut off any excess wrapping wire.

STEP 2

Cut a new piece of US 26-gauge (0.4mm) wire about 28in (700mm) long. Wrap this around the base of the flower twice and bring it to the front between two petals.

STEP 3

Thread on a seed bead and wrap the wire five times around one side of the petal. Add a crystal, seed bead, crystal, and another seed bead then wrap the wire around the opposite side of the petal about 14 times (this may need to vary so the rows sit equally). Add three seed beads and three crystals alternately for the next row. Wrap the wire around the opposite edge 14 times. String on enough seed beads and crystals to fit comfortably inside the petal. These petals have 11 rows of beads and you add more beads as the petal gets fatter, then reduce the crystals as you get to the point. Put beads on the wire and see if they fit before wrapping the wire around the opposite edge of the petal. Take them off and start again if they don't fit.

STEP 4

A 28in (700mm) piece of US 26-gauge (0.4mm) wire should be enough to fill one petal. When you get to the point of the petal, coil the wire a few times and cut off any excess with side cutters. Press the end of the wire against the petal wire edge so it's not sticking out and sharp.

STEP 5

It's impossible to keep the rows of beads perfectly in line, but do your best as it does make a difference to how it looks overall. Repeat Step 2 and 4 to completely fill all five petals.

STEP 6

When all the petals are complete, use a tiny amount of superglue on each coil so they stay in place when the tiara is being worn. To add the glue successfully, move the coil to one side add a tiny drop of glue to the petal wire and push the coil back over it. Make sure that it's in the right place as the glue goes hard very fast and then the coil is stuck fast.

STEP 7

Turn the flower over so the back is facing you and use a pair of chain-nose pliers to put a small right-angle bend in each wire, just enough to place the tiara band in. Bend the wire right up against the wrapped section.

STEP 8

Pick up the tiara band and shape it (see page 21) so it is comfortable to wear. Place it in between the wires and check it's a snug fit. Cut both wire ends off about 1½in (40mm) away from the band. It's much easier to work with short wires here.

STEP 9

Wrap the wire ends around the tiara band. Go around the band about three times; you will need to use chain-nose pliers to help as you won't be able to pull the wire tight enough with your fingers. If the petals are getting in your way, gently push them away.

STEP 10

If you've moved any petals in Step 9, then push them back into place and check they all look even. With your fingers and thumbs and using both hands, gently bend the petals into a curved shape by bending the petal over the top of your first finger. These petals are big enough that you can curve them down in the middle and tweak the end back up, which gives a nice appearance.

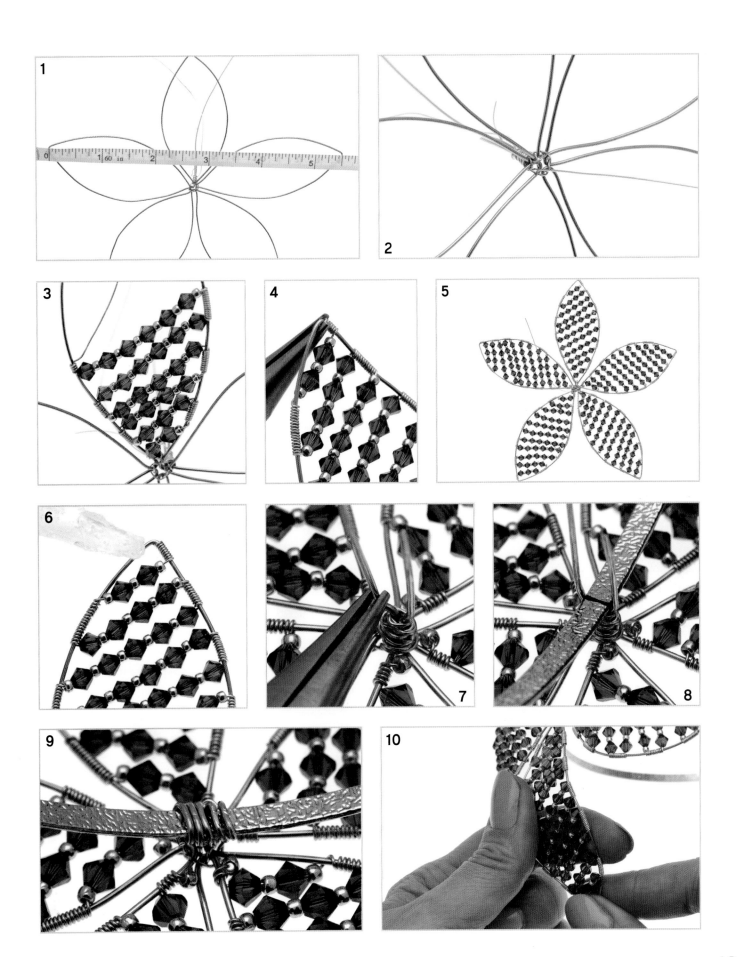

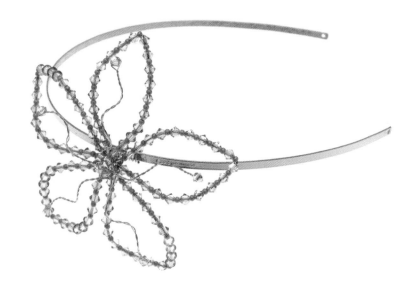

CRYSTAL-EDGE FLOWER SIDE TIARA

The flower on this tiara has a finished size of 4in (100mm), but it can be as big as you want it—just by adding more crystals. If you want a flower larger than about 6in (150mm) across, make sure you use US 18-gauge (1mm) wire. You will also need to check the size of the holes in the beads.

You will need

1 x roll of US 20-gauge (0.8mm) gold-colored wire
1 x roll of US 26-gauge (0.4mm) gold-colored wire
105 x 4mm pale gold crystal bicones
10g x 1.8mm (size 11) frosted gold seed beads
1 x gold-colored tiara band
Beading mat
Superglue
Masking tape
Chain-nose pliers
Medium bail-making pliers or round-nose pliers
Side cutters

STEP 1

Make a crystal-edge flower by following the technique on pages 122–3, using 20 seed beads and 20 crystals per flower (10 on each side of the petal). You will need to cut a length of three coils for this flower. When you have completed this you will have a long piece of US 26-gauge (0.4mm) wire waiting to be used; bring this between two petals and add a crystal. About 2in (50mm) away from the flower, bend the wire and trap the crystal. Twist the two wire ends together all the way down to the flower. This makes a crystal stamen.

STEP 2

Take a pair of bail-making pliers and wrap the twisted wire around the larger jaw. If you don't have bail-making pliers, wrap the twisted wire around one of the jaws of a pair of round-nose pliers. Make an open spiral on the wire. If you have enough wire left, bring it up between the next two petals and repeat Step 1 to make another crystal stamen. Wrap the wire end around the base of the flower a couple of times and cut off any excess. For the other three stamens you will need to add more wire. Cut a fresh piece of US 26-gauge (0.4mm) wire and wrap it a few times around the base of the flower to anchor the wire. Bring the wire up between two petals and repeat these steps to make a further three stamens.

STEP 3

You should have one stamen between each petal. When you have finished the stamens, bring the wire end on the last one to the back of the flower. After you have curved all five stamens, bring the wire end that is sitting at the back of the flower through the middle. Add three crystals to the US 26-gauge (0.4mm) wire and bring the wire back through the middle, pull tight to trap the crystals in the center of the flower. Wrap the free end around the base a few times and cut off any excess wire. Press the wire end into the coil.

STEP 4

Take the masking tape off the two wires at the bottom of the flower and bend them out at right angles away from each other right above the wrapped section. This is fairly easy to do with your fingers, but use chain-nose pliers if you wish.

STEP 5

Take a tiara band and shape it (see page 21) so it's comfortable to wear. Measure about 4¾in (120mm) up from one end of the band and place the flower against it with the wires facing outward, away from the band. Wrap the wire ends around the tiara band a few times and cut off any excess wire. Press the ends into the band so they sit flat. Add a little superglue if desired so that the ends don't catch on any hair.

STEP 6

Take a final look at the flower and gently bend the petals into a slight curve with your fingers. They won't move much as the crystals restrict it, but a slight curve gives the flowers a more natural look. Move the stamens around so that they sit nicely over each flower.

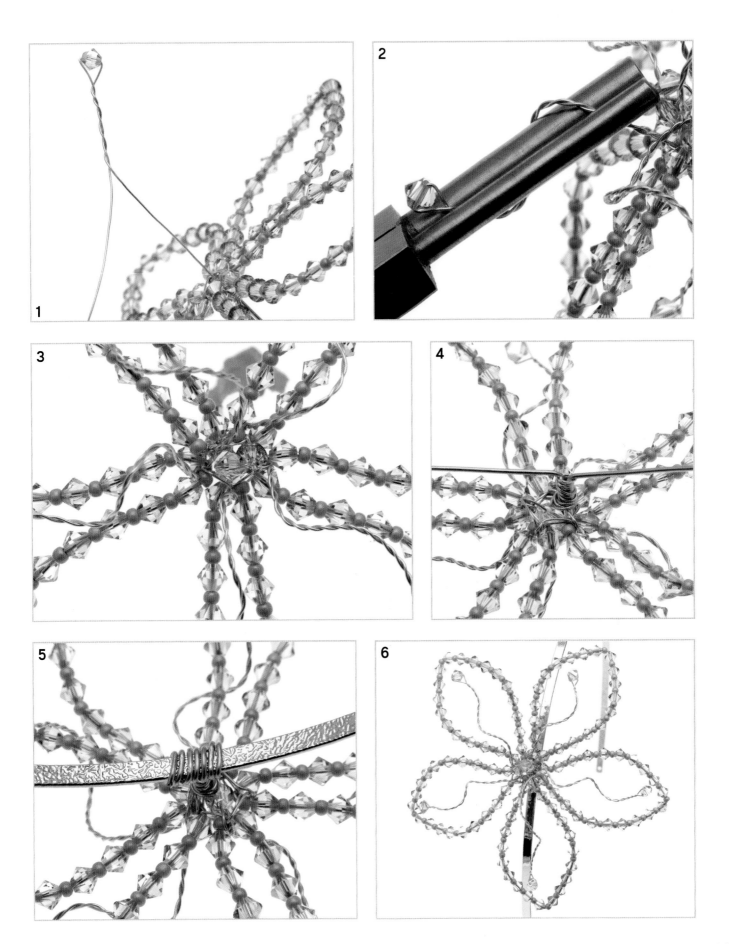

HAIRPIN

This pretty crystal hairpin has the smallest size of flower you can make using 4mm crystals. The flower can be wired onto a standard hairpin or bobby pin (kirby grip).

You will need

- 1 x roll of US 20-gauge (0.8mm) gold-colored wire
- 1 x roll of US 26-gauge (0.4mm) gold-colored wire
- 60 x 4mm pale gold crystal bicones
- 1 x 6mm pale gold crystal bicone
- 10g x 1.8mm (size 11) frosted gold seed beads
- Hairpin or bobby pin (kirby grip)
- Beading mat
- Superglue
- Masking tape
- Chain-nose pliers
- Round-nose pliers
- Side cutters
- Tape measure

STEP 1

Make a crystal-edge flower by following the technique on pages 122–3, using 12 seed beads and 12 crystals per flower (6 on each side of the petal). You will need to cut a length of two coils for this flower. Once complete, you will have a finished flower and a long piece of US 26-gauge (0.4mm) wire ready to use in Step 3.

STEP 2

Gently curve the petals slightly with your fingers. They won't curve a lot, but it's nice to have a little curve on each one.

STEP 3

Bring the US 26-gauge (0.4mm) wire through the middle of the flower to the front and thread on the 6mm crystal. Take the wire back down through the middle to the back of the flower. Pull the wire tight so that the crystal sits in the flower center. Wrap the wire end a couple of times around the wrapped stem and leave the wire end free.

STEP 4

On the back of the flower, measure 4in (100mm) beyond the wrapped stem and cut off the excess wire with side cutters.

STEP 5

Using chain-nose and round-nose pliers, make the wire ends into the same shape as the top of the hairpin.

STEP 6

If you have enough wire left on the end from Step 3, then use that to wrap the flower to the hairpin on one side. Hold the hairpin against the shaped stem and wrap the US 26-gauge (0.4mm) wire around both until you have covered the whole piece of stem wire. Cut a fresh piece of US 26-gauge (0.4mm) wire and wrap around the flower base a couple of times then down the other side of the hairpin. Add superglue to the ends so that they don't catch on any hair.

STEP 7

Take the chain-nose pliers and grasp the wrapped stem on the back of the flower. Bend gently but firmly until the flower sits parallel to the hairpin. This is the best angle for the flowers to sit in the hair as the pins can slide into any pinned-up hairstyle with the flower sitting flat against the hair. The finished size of the hairpin is 2½in (60mm).

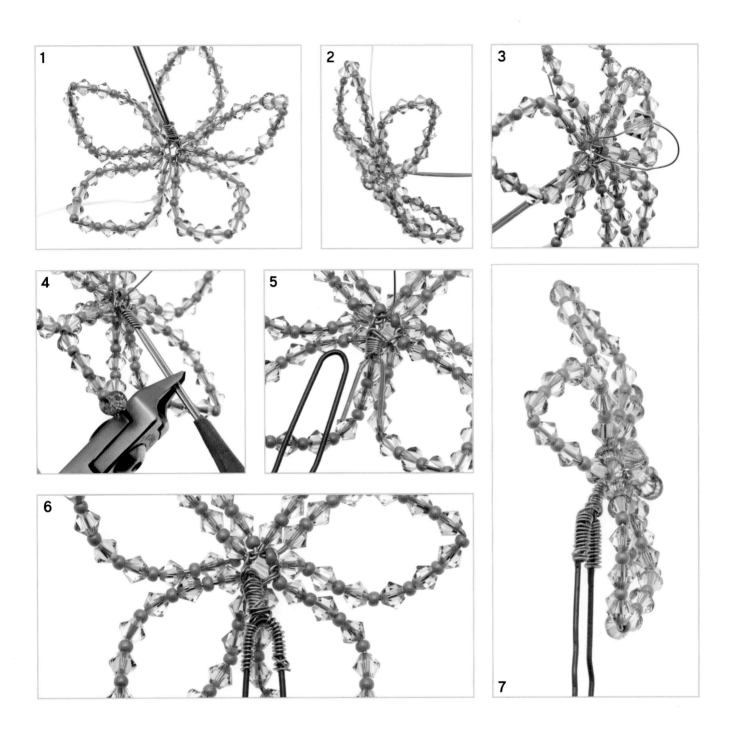

BRACELET

This beautiful flower is a good size for a bracelet in a corsage style as it just fills the wrist. The flower is 3¼in (80mm) in size, but if this is too big, then make a flower the same size as the hairpin on pages 132–3.

You will need

- 1 x roll of US 20-gauge (0.8mm) gold-colored wire
- 1 x roll of US 26-gauge (0.4mm) gold-colored wire
- 80 x 4mm pale gold crystal bicones
- 1 x 6mm pale gold crystal bicones
- 10g x 1.8mm (size 11) frosted gold seed beads
- 3ft (1m) x 1½in (40mm) wide gold organza ribbon
- Beading mat
- Superglue
- Masking tape
- Lighter or matches
- Chain-nose pliers
- Side cutters

STEP 1

Make a crystal-edge flower by following the technique on pages 122–3. Use 16 seed beads and 16 crystals per flower (8 on each side of the petal). You will need to cut a length of two coils for this flower. When you have completed this you will have a long piece of US 26-gauge (0.4mm) wire waiting to be used; bring this between two petals and wrap around the base of the flower stem to bind the two wires together.

STEP 2

Bring the wire up through the middle of the flower and thread on the 6mm crystal. Bring the wire down through the middle again and pull the wire tight so that the crystal sits in the middle of the flower. The crystal should be larger than the space in the middle of the flower so it will not drop through.

STEP 3

Wrap the wire around the stem a couple of times again and cut off the excess. Push the wire end flat against the wrapping with chain-nose pliers.

STEP 4

Cut the wire stems off about 2in (50mm) from the flower and bend them outwards away from each other. They need to be parallel with the flower.

STEP 5

Grasp the very end of one wire with round-nose pliers and make a spiral (see page 20). Roll the spiral up tight against the wrapped stem. Repeat for the other wire. These spirals will sit against the skin, so rub your finger across the finished spirals to make sure they are smooth with no sharp edges. If they feel a little sharp, add a drop of superglue to the wire.

STEP 6

Place your finger across the width of the petals and bend them gently into a slight curve as this shape sits better on the wrist. Tie a long piece of gold organza ribbon around the base of the flower between the spirals and the flower to make a wrap tie for the bracelet. Seal the ribbon ends by carefully heating with the flame from a lighter or match.

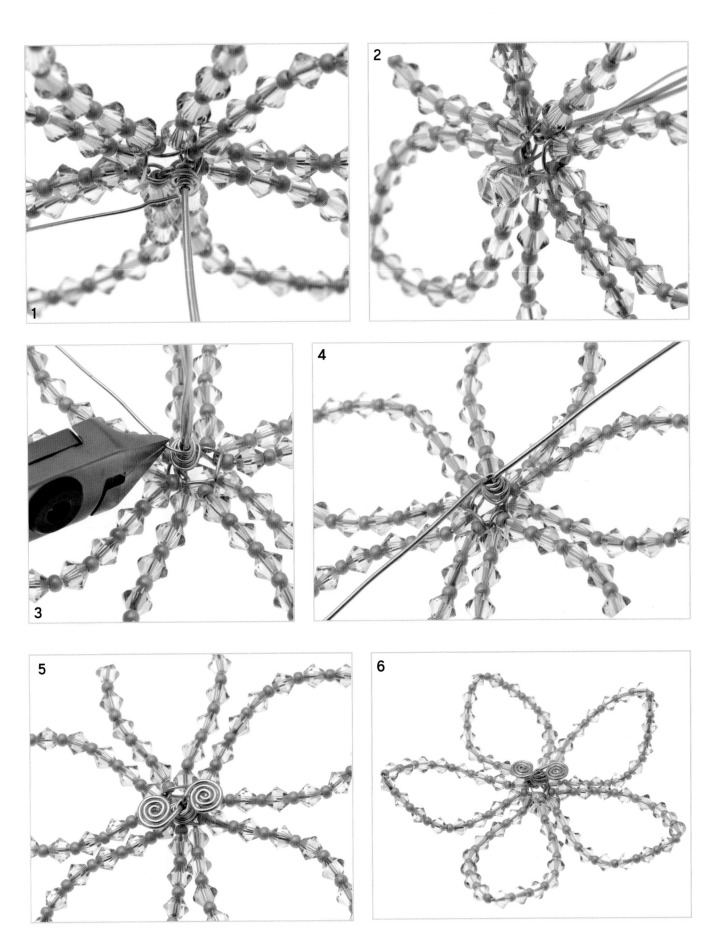

BROOCH

Sometimes you just want a little extra sparkle on a wedding outfit. This brooch will add a focal piece that can be pinned to a dress or lapel for extra color and interest.

You will need

1 x roll of US 20-gauge (0.8mm) gold-colored wire
1 x roll of US 26-gauge (0.4mm) gold-colored wire
80 x 4mm colored crystal bicones
10g x 1.8mm (size 11) gold seed beads
1 x 1in (25mm) gold-colored brooch bar
Beading mat
Superglue
Masking tape
Chain-nose pliers
Side cutters
Tape measure

STEP 1

Make a wire flower by following the technique on pages 120–21. You need to cut a length of two coils for this flower. The petal template needs to be 1½in (40mm) long. Bring the US 26-gauge (0.4mm) wire between two petals and wrap the wire around the flower stem wires six or more times, so the wires are securely tied together. Cut off any excess wrapping wire.

STEP 2

Cut a new piece of US 26-gauge (0.4mm) wire about 28in (700mm) long. Wrap this around the base of the flower twice and bring it to the front between two petals. Wrap the wire around the edge of one petal twice.

STEP 3

Thread on a seed bead and a crystal. Wrap the wire ten times around the other side of the petal. Add a crystal, seed bead, crystal, and another seed bead. Wrap the wire around the opposite side of the petal about eight times (this may need to vary so the rows sit equally).

STEP 4

Add a seed bead and then three crystals and seed beads alternately for the next row. Wrap the wire around the opposite edge eight times. The next row has four crystals and three seed beads. Then the rows go back down to match the bit already done. You'll need to wrap the wire about eight times between each row. Adjust the wrapping if the rows are not sitting evenly. A 28in (700mm) piece of US 26-gauge (0.4mm) wire will be more than enough to fill one petal. When you get to the point of the petal, coil the wire a few times and cut off any excess with side cutters. Press the end of the wire against the petal's wire edge so it's not sticking out and sharp.

STEP 5

Repeat Steps 3 and 4 to completely fill all five petals. Try to keep the petals even. If desired, you can glue the coils in place to hold the rows of beads, but you may find on the smaller flowers that it's not needed.

STEP 6

Turn the flower over so the back is facing you and bend both stem wires out at a right angle so they are parallel with the flower.

STEP 7

Using chain-nose pliers, bend the stem wires back on themselves so that the finished length is 1in (25mm), the same as the brooch bar. Use the bar as a measure if that helps.

STEP 8

Using the side cutters, snip off the wire ends where they cross over and then using chain-nose pliers move the ends in so they are in line with each other to make an oblong shape.

STEP 9

Cut a piece of US 26-gauge (0.4mm) wire and wrap around the base of the flower a couple of times so that it is secure. Open the brooch bar and place it over the oblong wire end you have just made. Bring the US 26-gauge (0.4mm) wire around the edge of the bar and through the hole in the brooch bar. Bring the wire around the outside of the brooch bar, making sure the wire is around the outside of the oblong shape. Thread the wire through the middle of the bar again. Go around and through the middle of the bar three times on each side of both holes. Finish with the wire between the brooch bar and the flower. Wrap the end around the base of the flower a few times and cut off any excess.

STEP 10

With your fingers and thumb gently bend the petals into a curved shape by bending each petal over the top of your first finger.

STEP 11

The finished size of this flower is 3¼in (80mm). The flower looks best with a good curve on the petals, which stops the ends of the petals getting caught on the fabric of a dress or coat.

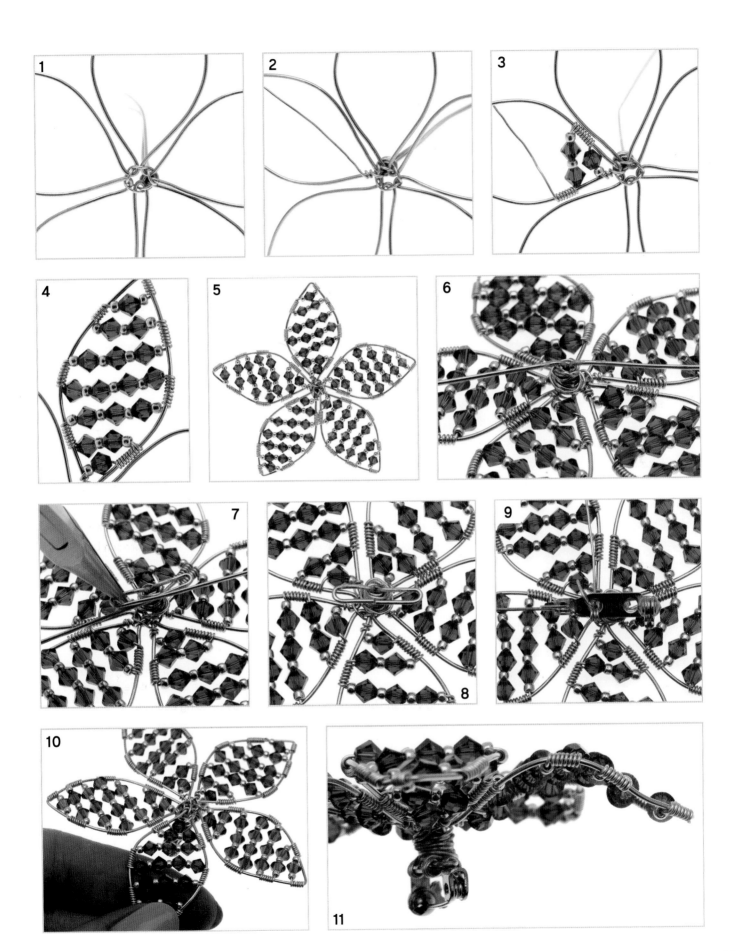

SHOE CLIPS

These little clips are lovely shoe decorations, designed to make a pair of wedding shoes shine. Each of these flowers is less than 2in (50mm) in size.

You will need

- 1 x roll of US 20-gauge (0.8mm) gold-colored wire
- 1 x roll of US 26-gauge (0.4mm) gold-colored wire
- 30 x 4mm colored (of your choice) crystal bicones
- 10g x 1.8mm (size 11) gold seed beads
- 2 x shoe clips
- Gold beading thread
- Beading needle
- Beading mat
- Superglue
- Masking tape
- Chain-nose pliers
- Round-nose pliers
- Side cutters

STEP 1

Make a wire flower by following the technique on pages 120–21. You need to cut a length of two coils for this flower. The petal template needs to be ¾in (19mm) long. Bring the US 26-gauge (0.4mm) wire between two petals and wrap the wire around the flower stem wires a few times so the flower is securely tied together.

STEP 2

Bring the US 26-gauge (0.4mm) wire through the middle of the flower and wrap it around the edge of a petal twice. Add a crystal and wrap it around the opposite edge of the petal six times.

STEP 3

Add a seed bead, crystal, then another seed bead and wrap the wire around the edge six times. The next row has a crystal, seed bead, then a crystal. Each row has about six wraps before the next row starts. As these flowers are small, it's a bit of a squeeze to get all the crystals in, but just push down the row before to allow room for the next row. When you get to the point of the petal, coil the wire a few times and cut off any excess with side cutters. Press the end of the wire against the petal wire edge so it's not sticking out and sharp.

STEP 4

Each petal needs a new piece of wire that's about 12in (305mm) long. Wrap the wire around the base of the flower a couple of times before bringing it up through the middle of the flower to start the petal, then repeat Steps 2 and 3 for each petal.

STEP 5

On the back of the flower bend both stem wires in the same direction so they are parallel with the flower. Tweak them out a bit with chain-nose pliers and then use round-nose pliers to curve the ends back toward the flower middle.

STEP 6

The length of the section in Step 5 needs to be the same as the shoe clip, so use the clip as your measurement guide. Snip off the wire ends.

STEP 7

Use beading thread to attach the shoe clips, as it is stronger than the wire. Thread up a needle and double the thread. Make a knot and take the needle through a hole in the shoe clip. Bring the needle in between the two threads and pull tight.

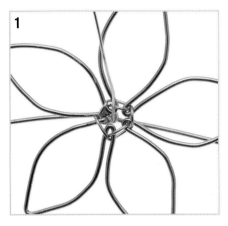

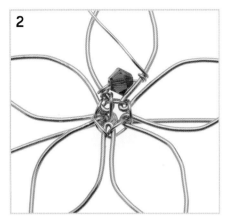

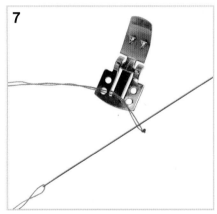

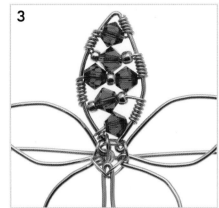

STEP 8

Place the clip on top of the flower and sew through the clip and around the edge, catching the wire back as you go. Use both holes on both sides of the clip and sew through each one multiple times. Knot the thread and cut off the excess.

STEP 9

Add a small amount of superglue over the sewn thread to make sure it is secure. Repeat the steps to make a shoe clip for the other shoe.

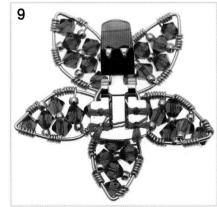

RESOURCES

UK

Beads Unlimited
PO Box 1
Hove
East Sussex BN3 5SG
Tel: +44 (0)1273 740777
www.beadsunlimited.co.uk

Beads Direct Ltd
10 Duke Street
Loughborough
Leicestershire LE11 1ED
Tel: +44 (0)1509 218028
www.beadsdirect.co.uk

The Bead Shop
44 Higher Ardwick
Manchester M12 6DA
Tel: +44 (0)161 274 4040
www.the-beadshop.co.uk

The Bead Shop (Nottingham) Ltd
7 Market Street
Nottingham NG1 6HY
Tel: +44 (0)115 9588899
www.mailorder-beads.co.uk

Fred Aldous Ltd
37 Lever Street
Manchester M1 1LW
Tel: +44 (0)161 236 4224
www.fredaldous.co.uk

Palmer Metals Ltd
401 Broad Lane
Coventry CV5 7AY
Tel: +44 (0)845 644 9343
www.palmermetals.co.uk

Spoilt Rotten Beads
7 The Green
Haddenham
Ely
Cambridgeshire CB6 3TA
Tel: +44 (0)1353 749853
www.spoiltrottenbeads.co.uk

Jillybeads
1 Anstable Road
Morecambe LA4 6TG
Tel: +44 (0)1524 412728
www.jillybeads.co.uk

The Bead Merchant
PO Box 5025
Coggeshall
Essex CO6 1HW
Tel: +44 (0)1376 570022
www.beadmerchant.co.uk

Bead Aura
3 Neal's Yard
Covent Garden
London WC2H 9DP
Tel: +44 (0)207 836 3002
www.beadaura.co.uk

The Genuine Gemstone
Company Limited
Unit 2D Eagle Road
Moons Moat
Redditch
Worcestershire B98 9HF
www.jewellerymaker.com
0800 6444 655

Creative BeadCraft
Unit 2 Asheridge Business
Centre
Asheridge Road
Chesham
Bucks HP5 2PT
01494 778818
www.creativebeadcraft.co.uk

Bijoux Beads
Elton House
2 Abbey Street
Bath BA1 1NN
Tel: +44 (0)1225 482024
www.bijouxbeads.co.uk

G J Beads
Unit L
St Erth Industrial Estate
Hayle
Cornwall TR27 6LP
Tel: +44 (0)1736 751070
www.gjbeads.co.uk

Beadsisters
Mid Cairngarroch Croft
Stoneykirk
Stranraer
Wigtownshire DG9 9EH
Tel: +44 (0)1776 830352
www.beadsisters.co.uk

Shiney Company
14 Sandy Park Road
Brislington
Bristol BS4 3PE
Tel: +44 (0)117 300 9800
www.shineyrocks.co.uk

Wires.co.uk
Unit 3 Zone A
Chelmsford Road Industrial
Estate
Great Dunmow
Essex CM6 1HD
Tel: +44 (0)1371 238013
www.wires.co.uk

Kernowcraft Rocks & Gems Ltd
Penwartha Road
Bolingey
Perranporth
Cornwall TR6 0DH
Tel: +44 (0)1872 573888
www.kernowcraft.com

Bead House
Quarmby Mills
Tanyard Road, Oakes
Huddersfield HD3 4YP
Tel: +44 (0)1484 485111
www.beadhouse.co.uk

Worldwide

Fire Mountain Gems and Beads
1 Fire Mountain Way
Grants Pass
OR 97526-2373
Tel: toll free 1-800-355-2137
Tel: from UK 1-541-956-7890
www.firemountaingems.com

Beadin' path
Tel: from UK 1-207-650-1557
www.beadinpath.com

Shipwreck Beads
8560 Commerce Place Dr
NE Lacey
WA 98516
Tel: from UK 1-360-754-2323
Tel: toll free 1-800-950-4232
www.shipwreckbeads.com

Fusion Beads
3830 Stone Way
N Seattle
WA 98103
Tel: from UK 1-206-781-9500
Tel: toll free 1-888-781-3559
www.fusionbeads.com

ACKNOWLEDGEMENTS

GMC Publications would like to thank the stylist, Jeni Dodson, and Circe De La Rosa of MOT Models. Also a big thank you to Carla Day-Rolfe, Dominique Page and Judith Chamberlain for their help with props and accessories.

INDEX

To order a book, or to request a catalog, contact:
GMC Publications Ltd, Castle Place, 166 High Street, Lewes,
East Sussex, BN7 1XU, United Kingdom
Tel: +44 (0)1273 488005   www.gmcbooks.com